HOUSE WHISPER

HOUSE WHISPER

Energies of Man, Places and Spaces

Georg Peterseil

AuthorHouse™ UK Ltd.
1663 Liberty Drive
Bloomington, IN 47403 USA
www.authorhouse.co.uk
Phone: 0800.197.4150

© 2014 Georg Peterseil. All rights reserved.

No part of this book may be reproduced, stored in a retrieval system, or transmitted by any means without the written permission of the author.

Published by AuthorHouse 09/22/2014

ISBN: 978-1-4969-8762-4 (sc)
ISBN: 978-1-4969-8763-1 (e)

Cover Photo by Georg Peterseil

This book is printed on acid-free paper.

Because of the dynamic nature of the Internet, any web addresses or links contained in this book may have changed since publication and may no longer be valid. The views expressed in this work are solely those of the author and do not necessarily reflect the views of the publisher, and the publisher hereby disclaims any responsibility for them.

In gratitude to
the Spirit of the Earth
and all my Teachers

CONTENTS

INTRODUCTION IX

PART I
THE BRIDGE FROM THE MATERIAL
WORLD TO ENERGY 1

1. MY LIFE'S JOURNEY 11
2. OPENING THE SENSES 20
3. AWARENESS OF BELIEFS 28
4. AWAKENING THE SOUL 33
5. RAISING THE FREQUENCY OF
   OUR ENERGY FIELD 45

PART II
PLACES AND SPACES 63

6. BLOCKED ENERGIES AND THEIR HEALING 75
7. ENERGIES ON A PERSONALITY LEVEL 84
8. ENERGIES OF HIGHER FREQUENCY 99
9. HOME 126

ENDNOTES 129

INTRODUCTION

*...this world is a projection of events
in a deeper realm of reality.*

David Bohm

*The question that sometimes drives me hazy:
Am I or the others crazy?*

Albert Einstein

How can I introduce a subject as alien to our thinking as energies in places and buildings, especially, as I do not mean devices powered by oil or wind or solar energy? When I say energy I do not mean these technical energies which bring comfort into our homes and connect us to the world.

I am referring to energies which are in us and all around us. These energies allow our heart to pump and our lungs to breath and, at a subtler level allow us to think and to feel. When we are connected to these energies, we become aware of our behaviour, feelings and thinking and why we choose particular thoughts. We also gain access to our creative energies through this connection.

INTRODUCTION

With the help of these subtle energies we also choose the place where we live. You may be living in a rented apartment or own a house. You may live in a mobile home or be homeless under a bridge. You may go on holidays in a tent or a hotel room. You may even make your living designing, building or selling houses. Whatever your situation, you are always in a place and will always be surrounded by space.

And yet how often are we aware of the place we have chosen to inhabit, even if only for a moment? Have you ever thought of getting in contact with a place as a way of communicating with it or even creating a relationship with it? When we enter a room we are keen to find our own place. When we are with a group of people we long to belong. In fact, we spend our whole lives longing to find our place in this world and a sense of belonging to it.

When we lived in agriculturally-based societies, we were strongly connected to a specific place. We had an intimate relationship with the place because our livelihood depended on this connection. The culture we created came from and in cooperation with the land. With the advent of the industrial revolution and the subsequent move to cities, we became uprooted, thus losing our connection with the earth and with a specific place which had given us our identity as a member of a family and a community. The metropolitan culture which arose and is still growing, along with an emerging global culture, uproot us even more. The latter replaces a sense of natural place with a virtual space. Our need to be connected to a real place is more necessary now than ever before. In an age in which we can fly into our solar system and observe even the lighting of a cigarette via satellite, it is time to start our inner journey into the vast universe of our inner spaces.

In order to feel rooted wherever we are, we need to connect to the place and the spirit of the earth. Once we are connected, the light from above (universal energy) and the light from below (earth energy) merge and become one. Because we are connected to our centre within, we feel at home where ever we are. Finding this home in yourself is the ultimate aim and hope of this book.

As a young architect I designed houses, focusing on the external beauty of houses through the materials, shapes and colours. When I built my own house and got to know myself better, I learned that a house is not the same as a home. It is the relationship between ourselves and the spirit of a place that transforms a house and place into a home.

A musician creates an intimate relationship with his instrument, a singer with her voice, an IT-specialist with her computer and a fisherman with the sea. I as an architect choose to create this deeper relationship with houses and places. Whatever we love passionately, brings us home to ourselves.

I focus on houses and family homes in this book as this was my main focus as an architect. However, once we understand the basic principles of connection, they can be widened to the spirit of towns and cities, to the spirit of family or an organisation or company, or any task we are engaged in.

We cannot think our way into energy. The only way to connect to energy is by feeling into it. To help you learn how to feel into energies, I provide you with an exercise at the end of each chapter. I hope these exercises serve you well and enable you to understand this book with your heart rather than your head. Let us begin with the first exercise below.

EXERCISE

For the next twenty minutes, go into a space where you are undisturbed. Sit down in a comfortable position. Take a few deep breaths. Relax your whole body starting from your feet, then your calves, your knees and thighs, your buttocks and your whole torso from belly to chest, your arms and shoulders, your neck and at last your head. Feel your whole body being relaxed. Next visualise your whole body as air. There are no boundaries between your body and the surrounding air. You and your surroundings are one. There is no separation. You are the centre of an energy field containing intelligence and power. You are the energy. Feel this energy. Everything you need to know is available to you right now. If any images come, acknowledge them and let them go. After a few minutes of being in this silent, apparently empty space, bring your focus back to your body. Feel the floor under your feet, then start to move your feet, legs, torso, shoulders, arms and head. Take a deep breath and slowly open your eyes. Look around. How do you feel?

I suggest you repeat this exercise once a day over the next two days.

PART I
THE BRIDGE FROM THE MATERIAL WORLD TO ENERGY

*In the West today the masculine aspect,
the rational, active, aggressive
power of the mind is dominant,
while in the east the feminine aspect,
the intuitive, passive, sympathetic
power of the mind is dominant.
The future of the world depends on
the "marriage" of those two minds,
the conscious and the unconscious,
the rational and the intuitive,
the active and the passive.*

Bede Griffiths

Historical background

Indigenous peoples all over the planet have always had a very intimate relationship with the place and the area in which they live. Their livelihood and survival depended on this close contact. Shamans, Medicine Men, High Priests, Druids and whatever else they were called all over the globe connected with otherworldly powers to heal, to find a source of water, a safe place to rest or wild animals to hunt for food.

THE BRIDGE FROM THE MATERIAL WORLD TO ENERGY

To talk about energy within us and our environment is uncommon in today's western culture. And yet the subject of energy is as old as the Chinese teachings of Feng Shui [1] or Vastu Shastra[2] (the Indian Science of dwellings). It also features in the practice of Geomancy and Shamanism.

Shamanism[3] is a traditional practice which perceives the entire universe as alive and interconnected. According to the 'Scandinavian Center for Shamanic Studies' "everything that has life also has spirit and power...Here power should be understood in the sense of 'energy', not to be confused with 'might'." Geomancy[4], meaning divination from Earth originated in Arabia. According to *Mid-Atlanitic Geomancy,* geomancy explores the realm where human consciousness meets and dialogues with the Spirit of the Earth.

All these teachings are based on the notion that the earth is alive. We all live in a place and my experience tells me that the place in which we live and the space we inhabit and call our home mirrors parts of ourselves. I do not believe that the place in which we live is a random coincidence. The place we were drawn to in the first place can either support us in our well-being, or, if we are not aware of its energetic quality, be destructive.

Quantum Physics

When we try to understand my experiences of working with the energies of places and spaces within a materialistic world view, none of it makes any sense. It will seem weird at best and outrageously crazy at worst. We must be willing to widen our perception. We need to dare to fly and trust that we do not fall, even though all our experiences tell us that gravity will pull us back down. But if we do not identify with our bodies, we will learn that there is more to life than we ever dreamed possible.

While we in the western world live predominantly according to a materialistic world view, quantum physics[5] makes us aware of a subatomic world of energy and matter, wave and particle. We know from the findings of quantum physics that the subatomic world constantly switches from wave to particle and back to wave, thus opening a world of probability. In this world pure energy can manifest in seemingly rigid material form only to disintegrate back to energy again. This means that the overwhelming majority of reality is invisible energy, which manifests at times as physical reality. A place or a building exist both on an energetic and a physical level; as wave and as particle.

Karen Kingston in 'Creating Sacred Space with Feng Shui' writes that the Balinese live in these two worlds: in the material, visible world and the metaphysical, unseen world of energy and vibration.

If we only perceive the material, physical world, we only see a tiny part of a much wider reality. We operate only in this time-space dimension, instead of in a vast multidimensional reality. According to quantum physics, this invisible reality makes up more than 90% of reality. This apparently empty space is energy containing intelligence, power, compassion and a unifying glue we call love. How can we attempt to understand this world and our place in it, if we only focus on less than 10% of reality and believe this to be the whole of reality?

THE BRIDGE FROM THE MATERIAL WORLD TO ENERGY

Inner Journey

Old traditions all over the globe perceived reality as both physical and metaphysical, and quantum physics confirms this. So how can we regain knowledge of the invisible part of reality? We always first access this invisible part of reality inside ourselves, may it be conscious or unconscious. We then see this inner reality mirrored outside of us in the world. The conscious inner journey into our own universe is a continuing journey into the unknown, into the depths of our inner worlds. Let us take the example of looking at a building. First we see the colours, proportions and materials. Now let us go beyond the surface to the grain of sand in the mortar, still deeper to the molecules, then the atoms, electrons, neutrons and protons and beyond to the vast spaces between them.

The deeper we go inside ourselves, the more we are able to see these invisible layers of reality reflected all around us. The place in which we live provides a mirror of our own energy field. The deeper we look into this mirror, the better we get to know ourselves. This book is about this inner journey of discovering our inner senses which give us access to these inner worlds of energy. Today some of us are excited to see a film in three dimensions. What if we would carry in us the potential to go into four, five, six, seven or more dimensions?

This focusing on our inner life, i.e. our thoughts and feelings, opens up a wider reality. In this wider, multi-dimensional reality everything is filled with intelligence and power and a desire to communicate and connect. Instead of seeing ourselves as separate from our environment, I suggest that we can enter into an intimate relationship with the building in which we live and its place. When we open and develop our inner senses, our sense of separation is transformed into connection. The place we feel drawn to, becomes a mirror of our own inner landscape. "We against the world" now becomes "We in co-operation with the world". We become co-creators with the world around us: our home supports us and we support the place in which we live. It is the end of perceiving ourselves as isolated from our surroundings.

Essence

Through all my encounters with places, I have learned that places and buildings are alive. Their energy field contains information which helps us see problems with a wider and more inclusive perspective. This is how we can solve problems and understand situations with a clarity gained by perceiving the whole of a situation.

In order to perceive the whole, we need to switch to another wave length in our brain, tune into another frequency and change our mind. The secret is in the energy frequencies. With our eyes we can only see a certain band of frequencies. With our ears we can only hear a very limited band of frequencies. So, to widen our perception of reality, we have to go beyond our limited sense of reality. We cannot find a multi-dimensional reality out there with our five outer senses. Instead we have to develop our inner senses-which are much more than a sixth sense. We need to feel into the situation, into the space or place. When we do this, the boundaries between me as the observer and the house or place seen as an object disappear.

We experience a union, a live communication resulting in a mutually supportive relationship. The relationship unfolds in the space between the place and us humans, between object and observer. Or better still: the object and the observer are transformed into this relationship. Two separate, material entities transform into something invisible. This invisible relationship is what I call the energy, spirit or essence of a place or building.

I am in no doubt that outstanding examples of architecture demonstrate that the architect intuitively connected with the spirit of the place. The most prominent example of the building and the place being in communication and in harmony with each other is for me Frank Lloyd Wright's *Fallingwater* in Western Pennsylvania in the United States. The clients had suggested to view the waterfall from their house. But the architect envisaged the house 'hanging' over the waterfall.

Separate reinforced concrete "trays" are dramatically cantilevered over the stream to form the living and bedroom levels. When I stood there in the centre of the living room, I felt as if the water underneath would sweep me off my feet, saying: "Life is in constant flow. Don't hold on, let go, let go; every moment is fresh and new". Its large single glazed windows allow the surrounding forest, the river below and sky above to become one with the inner space. Edgar Kaufman, jr., the owner's son, remarked: "(the house) itself (is) an ever-flowing source of exhilaration, (...) spouting nature's endless energy and grace. House and site together form the very image of man's desire to be at one with nature, equal and wedded to nature."[6]

From my experience there are an increasing number of people who are sensitive to energy blocks in houses. The occupants ask diviners or energy workers to clear the energies, to detect underground waterways or geopathic lines (stress or fault lines in the earth). The occupants are then advised where to position the bed or how to stop energy seeping out of the room. This method is certainly of value, but it only looks at pieces of a jigsaw. My aim instead is to look at the whole picture, to get in contact with the spirit of the place, the genius loci, the blueprint, the essential quality.

The basis of my work, which is supported by years of experience, is that details are contained in the essence, as the essence is whole and all-inclusive. Therefore I can draw on details whenever I need to in the unfolding process.

Proof

If you want proof of the existence of energy, then the images and insights are proof. The feeling of the energy is proof. The sum of coincidences and serendipity and a general sense of harmony that mirror the inner alignment and connection to the spirit of the place gives proof. If there would be some mechanically or electronically generated form of proof, the rational mind would be satisfied, but we would still be disconnected and experience ourselves as separate.

We ask and the energy responds. This request in form of an intention or question requires faith: faith that an answer will be given. If we need proof from an outside source, we can't develop faith in us. We may have had faith in our parents, in politicians or the church, but then we were disappointed. What do we do now? Do we put our trust in scientists, in gurus or pop stars or do we choose to develop faith in ourselves and in our own abilities?

So, can I provide scientific proof? No. Do I want to provide it? No. Even if I could, I wouldn't want to because we wouldn't gain anything. We cannot develop faith, if we need proof from an outside source. Energy is life force and life is a mystery. To enter the mystery is a personal inner journey and every one's journey is unique and different.

I suggest we perceive the space we inhabit as our partner, who holds up a mirror to show us both our strengths and our weaknesses. Just like the partner or children with whom we share our lives, we can also form an intimate relationship with the space and place in which we spend most of our time. We may live for decades in a house or apartment without ever entering into a conversation with its energies, and remain unconscious of the teachings, the cries for help, or offerings of healing and support which the place may have to give us.

In the first draft of this writing I tried to build a bridge between the rational mind and the soul; between the material and the energetic level; between the visible, touchable and the invisible non-graspable, between so called facts and fantasy; between the apparent objective and the personal experience. I tried to do this with the rational mind with models and explanations. But I realized that I get caught in endless arguments which are inevitable and inescapable at the level of the rational mind. I got caught in the duality of opposites, because I missed a central reference point which is above duality.

I decided to share my personal life story with you. The reason for telling you my own story of disconnection and separation is to encourage you to reconnect to yourself and the place you call 'home'.

When the earth and the other planets turn around the sun and the sun around the milky way and our galaxy around other galaxies, where is the still centre in all this movement, a reference point from which to describe my unique experiences other than from my own core? This book is therefore a personal view point, a personal experience shared with you. If we believe the findings of quantum physics, this universe is a hologram in which every grain of sand contains the whole. Similarly, my personal story becomes a shared story, when you read it with an open heart.

The aim of the following exercise is to bring you in contact with your inner centre.

EXERCISE:

Again choose a space where you will be undisturbed for the next twenty minutes. Sit in a comfortable position and close your eyes. Relax your whole body from toes to head as in the previous exercise. Now visualise again your whole body being air. You and your surroundings are one. There is no separation. Extend your space, including the whole house or apartment. Now visualise all the walls and ceilings dissolve into thin air. The boundaries of floors, basement and roof disappear. You are now one with your surroundings. Become aware that you are the centre of a field of energy. If images appear, acknowledge them and let them go. After a few minutes of resting in this space, bring your awareness back to the room and then to your body. Feel your feet on the ground and your buttocks on the chair. Start to move your body and slowly return to this physical reality. How do you feel? If you had any experiences in this space, you may want to write them down.

1. MY LIFE'S JOURNEY

*We cannot discover new lands
without losing sight of the shore
for a long time*

Andre Gide

I was born in Vienna, Austria, soon after the Second World War. This meant I was born into a world of ruins and rebuilding, of chaos and frantic survival, of guilt and denial. I laid myself across the birth channel in my mother's womb and had to be pulled out with tongs by force. I like to see this as an act of defiance against entry into this world.

As my mother soon after became pregnant again she felt I had to grow up fast. After 10 months I was weaned off nappies, which at that time were of cotton and had to be washed by hand. I could sit on a pot, walk and talk much earlier than most babies. My early life was a frantic fight for survival in a home of increasing conflicts, often violent, between my parents. When my father's business collapsed, I collapsed too. I thought: 'this is too much, I can't cope with this'. I was suddenly paralyzed as I sat on the potty and had to be rushed off to hospital. I was clinically dead for some minutes, when I was told by a higher entity to return to my body as I would be looked after.

While I was able to walk and move again, my resentment towards my mother was so strong that I refused to speak to her for another year. During that year I only talked to my baby sister. When I eventually talked again, I had a stutter and was very shy and withdrawn.

Even though the situation at home and in my surroundings had not changed, I had a strong will to survive and found comfort in withdrawing into myself. Despite my stutter and shyness I was good in school and interested in learning. By the age of eight or nine I made a conscious decision to use learning and education as a way to escape the perceived hell of constant fighting between my parents. I also loved to draw and paint and make things with my hands, which provided a form of escape as well as a connection through the imagination with my soul.

My life started to change after I made this decision. Life at home became more harmonious. At that time my father had an operation, I had whooping cough and did not see my parents for 6 weeks as I stayed with my aunt and my grandmother in the countryside. My father stopped drinking and my parents stopped fighting. I went to a higher level of secondary school with Latin and later Greek in the syllabus. I joined a youth club and loved to play soccer and go skiing. During the school holidays my family stayed at a farm in a then remote area in the South of Austria.

We played together with a group of other children from cities and helped the farmer by looking after the cattle and bringing food and drink to the fields during harvesting. Farming was still done with oxen and horses at the time. Bread was baked in a special stove, butter was churned, eggs collected and pigs and hens killed. The mothers cooked together in the big kitchen. During thunderstorms at night we huddled together in the living room in pyjamas (thunderstorms in the mountains being stronger and louder and more frightening than any I had ever experienced in Vienna). Harvesting was a communal activity that brought all the farmers from the neighbourhood together, while we children sat on top of cart loads of hay or sheaves of grain. I also loved to walk through the forests picking mushrooms and blueberries.

With the Youth Club we went on trips to the countryside, which involved making fires, listening to stories, sleeping in tents, playing thief and police in a forest at night, stealing maize from a field and being chased by the farmer, carrying the cross through a forest on Good Friday, listening to live classical music and learning to play the recorder. I would play the main character in a play and to this day I don't know how I managed that. Something in me started to stir and come to life again.

During puberty my shyness of girls and a deep sense of inferiority were compensated with smoking and an assumed air of superiority, which brought me more and more into the rational mind. As I was interested in both mathematics and art and crafts I decided to study architecture. I was mainly interested in the artistic side. The technical subjects I only managed through perseverance and hard work. My heart opened with joy and enthusiasm when I encountered famous examples of architecture on trips during my studies. But I never gained practical experience with the building process, tools or materials. I suppose I did not want to get my hands and clothes dirty.

After successfully finishing my studies, I felt I needed to get my hands and feet dirty. I worked as a supervisor on construction sites, ranging from tunnels to industrial buildings. I suffered more and more from stress as I tried to experience architecture from the builder's perspective and make a successful career. When my marriage failed unexpectedly, my life's dream fell apart. A dam of pent-up emotions, ranging from anger, rage and sadness to joy and happiness, burst open. I left my wife and our two children with her new partner, and spent some nights homeless, my car and a bag of clothes my only belongings. Other nights I spent with women. I began working in a design office and this became the most creative and fulfilling professional experience until then. I also started to write a diary, read a lot and sketch buildings, streets, places and faces.

The feelings of guilt, rage and sadness finally ended in the questions: "Who am I?" and "What is my purpose?". I ended all fleeting relationships with women and set out on a path of self-discovery. I felt in seventh heaven when I met Bettina, my current wife. Within a few months we moved-in together. I quit my job, which suddenly had lost its magic. We left Vienna and bought a small cottage in the Austrian country side. We were on a quest to find our roots and were living towards a self-sufficient life, keeping sheep, chickens and cats. We spun our own wool, baked bread, started a garden, listened to the deafening silence and marvelled at the starry night sky.

It was here that we first encountered Native American teaching, with its connection with and reverence for nature. For the first time in my life I worked with tools, bringing the house back to its original simplicity. This was also the first time I experienced a house coming alive. The house taught me to peel back the layers of false identities in myself as I scraped off layers of paint instead of putting on another layer on top of the old one. It taught me the essentials of life: relationships, connections, healthy food and practical clothes. It also taught me the importance of a home instead of success, pretence, money and fast cars. For the first time I felt rooted in myself and life was simple.

As I worked the land and spent time in the surrounding mountains and forests, my love for and connection with nature were reawakened. We fell into a rhythm with the seasons. In winter we wrote, read and sang, we split timber to fire our combined ceramic stove and range and fed the animals. In summer we eat outside, marvelled at the variety of wild flowers in the neighbouring meadows, made hay, planted and looked after the garden, harvested the fruits from the trees and went for long walks in the surrounding mountains, fields and forests.

I started to paint again, began recording my dreams or wrote fairy tales. When our daughter was born I started to learn to play the guitar. We bought a book of old country songs and sang at night by candle light or sat outside with fireflies lighting the mysterious dark. It was indeed a "Time of Miracles and Wonder" as Paul Simon would later sing.

After a few years and after having written a book about our experience, the house and place became too small. I felt a desire to get to the core of things and the root of problems and realized there were too many layers of culture around me and nothing more for me to do and learn in Austria. Inspired by Native American teachings, we longed to live in the wilderness. Open to move to any country in the world we landed a year later in the West of Ireland on a piece of bog land on top of a hill and next to a lake. The heather-covered land seemed empty to me, like a wet desert. There was no road, no electricity, no water, not a single tree and only one bush: a yellow flowering gorse bush. No one had lived in this area since the famine in the mid-19th century.

When a digger came onto the land to dig the road and the foundation for the house, I felt the turmoil in the landscape as much as in myself. There was a heap of turf not far from the road which belonged to a neighbour. We agreed to provide a passage way for him to his turf by covering some drains with pipes. After he and his brothers took their turf, they never greeted us again. We were so busy with building our home, we forgot about the matter. It was only years later that the significance of the situation became clear to us.

We started off living in a caravan, then built around it and finally moved the caravan to build the living room in its place. We got connected to electricity after two years and to water after three when the whole neighbourhood was connected to a water supply for the first time. As the whole process of building a house was new to me, I welcomed working without power tools. This allowed me to be attentive to detail. I learned the different skills as I went along: brick laying, carpentry, sheet metal work, etc. My impatience, fear and lack of trust, however, resurfaced intermittently and resulted in mistakes which I had to repair over the years, right up to the present. The house became a mirror of my inner state back then, reflecting my fears and faithlessness, my unwillingness to admitting that I didn't know the answer to a question, my righteousness and consequently not listening to others, as well as daring to venture creatively into unknown territory.

The house grew like a plant over a couple of years with one or two rooms added each year. A few months after we had moved into the half built house and the first feelings of euphoria had settled, I felt a darkness rising in me. Suddenly everything was alien. I could only connect to people superficially, I missed forests and the lush meadows and the wide variety of fruit and vegetables of Austria. There were no coffee houses and places where I could sit outside and watch people strolling or rushing past me. There were no cycling lanes or colourful, richly decorated buildings with baroque facades. I came here to get away from the cultural layers and reach the core of things. Now I missed those added layers. There was no cultural frosting on this cake. Instead it smelled of poverty and hardship.

While we focused on finishing the interior of the house, we started to unearth our whole belief system by questioning every belief that created unhappiness. We uncovered thousands of them. Parallel to the removal of the burdens on the land we became aware of burdens we had brought with us. They originated sometimes back a few generations and contained unfinished family business of failure, incest, alcoholism, betrayal, depression, etc. It was as if by digging up the bog we had brought all the darkness and stored memories the bog holds in its water saturated belly into the light. The form of the burdens from Austria (or in Bettina's case from Germany) was different, yet the energetic quality was the same. It was therefore directly reflected back to us. The level of inner war and tension became so strong that we decided to clear and drain our own inner bog of darkness and feelings of unhappiness by questioning our beliefs.

To create a space for this inner work we sold our car and decided to home-school our children. While we started off with the best intentions, the bad teacher and the bad father came to the surface very soon and old unresolved issues from past generations were now being acted out. At the same time my inner garden, which I saw on arrival reflected in the "wet desert" of the bog land, started to flourish as I played games with the children, sang, painted, wrote poetry, danced and acted.

As we started to feel the fruits of our inner work, the land around our home began to flourish. The place teemed with an abundant diversity of trees, bushes, flowers; wild animals and birds, including ducks, pheasants, frogs, hares, earth worms, sea gulls, swans and herons.

After withdrawing for years within our family and feeling much happier, we eventually wanted to connect our place and home to the community. But we felt something was holding us back. It was then that we asked a man to come and clear the energy of our place; and a lot of clearing needed to be done.

Weeks later I was introduced by a friend to shamanism. From the first day I had the feeling that this is something I have always known. I had only forgotten it and now it returned, like cycling after years without practice, but in my case it may have been after life times. I became a student, counsellor and practitioner of shamanism and started to use my connection to the earth when travelling as well as in my professional life.

In the last few years I have also started to practice a bio-energetic meditation[7]. This involves shaking the body to allow universal energy to flow through me, thereby clearing any areas of blocked energy, even releasing any energy still blocked from the time I was paralysed as a child and even before that.

I told my life story in brief for two reasons. Firstly to show you that I had to heal myself before I could heal the earth and release blocked energies in places and houses. The second reason is that I believe my life's journey from total paralysis to coming alive, from isolation to connecting to myself and my environment, from thinking to feeling could be a symbol for the challenges facing Western society.

EXERCISE:

For this exercise you will need to set aside between thirty minutes and an hour. Take a pen and paper and find a quiet place. Take a few deep breaths. When you feel comfortable, ask yourself if there is a thread weaving through your life and if yes, what is this thread? If you have difficulties finding the thread, I suggest that you dare to go into the unknown. Ask for help. If you believe in a higher being, ask that being. If not, I suggest that you set an intention that you will find the thread. Now just start writing. Give your inner critic a rest. Just keep writing without censoring the thoughts and feelings that come through.

When you are finished, read what you have written. Now draw the thread. Are there knots in the thread? Is the thread torn at a point in your life? Do you find meaning in your life's story? If you do not find the thread, stop looking and let go. It may appear "out of thin air" a few hours or days later. Maybe there is no thread, only what seems like chaos, only broken pieces. Can you accept this as your thread? What does it say about your life?

2. OPENING THE SENSES

*For too long we've ignored
the wild intelligence of our bodies,
taking our primary truths from technologies
that hold the living world at a distance.*

David Abram, Becoming Animal

Most of us are lucky enough to have five functioning senses: sight, hearing, touch, smell and taste. Our eyes, ears, fingers and toes, nose and tongue are the means to transmit outer stimuli into our brain and inform us about the world. I call these five senses our 'outer senses'.

When I studied and worked as an architect, I focused mainly on my eyes and the fingers of my right hand. As they took on the main workload of sensing the world, I needed glasses while my eyes were often tired. When I quit my job, my glasses became obsolete within a few weeks. I did not need them anymore as the other senses became more active and my eyes could relax.

The prime focus on my eyes had all started with the decision to give formal education my priority. To study and to become successful as an architect was to prove to the world that I could be successful, earn money, have an identity, and be someone. While I succeeded in that aspect, I failed in other areas and this resulted in a broken marriage. I believed "time is money", while rushing through life. I was good in arguing my case, good at pretending to be self-confident, good at playing "the game".

The break-up of the marriage and the separation from my two children showed me the narrow limits of my world view. My heart broke open, my emotions spilled over in a rollercoaster ride of feelings, jumping from joy to hate and from excitement to sadness. The crisis came to a climax one winter, when I felt deeply depressed and suicidal. Questions of "Who am I? What is this all about? What is my purpose?" emerged. I decided I finally wanted to get to know myself. I started to go to self-development groups and bio-dynamic meditations. Then I met Bettina and everything changed. Nothing which I had done before seemed to fit anymore. A radical change was required.

I sold most of my books and bought tools instead. I stopped reading and started writing instead. We painted together, invented stories and fairy tales spontaneously. We spent time in nature. I could not sit anymore for a whole day at a desk in an enclosed space. I needed to move in the fresh air. I quit work and felt drawn to live in the country side because living in a city had become meaningless for me.

Until I quit my job, my senses had been reduced to the fingers of my right hand touching a pencil and my eyes focusing on lines of ink on a large piece of paper. Now I was curious to get my hands dirty and my body sweating from digging the soil to put my first seeds in the ground. I would watch the first shoots come up. I marvelled at the smell of fresh carrots weeks later when I dug them up, washed them, cut them, smelled them, cooked them and tasted them.

I smelled manure from sheep and chickens and fresh earth after I dug and turned the sods. We bought a mill to grind grains of wheat and rye by hand. I kneaded the dough with my hands and enjoyed the smell and taste of fresh homemade bread.

I cleaned the existing pig sty to make room for sheep and chickens. In the summer time I cut the grass with a scythe and turned it until it was dried by the sun. We collected and saved the hay to feed the sheep in winter. We sheared the sheep, got the fleece washed and combed into wool to spin our own yarn and Bettina then knitted jumpers, hats and socks.

After I learned that the water came from a drain alongside the road, I discovered a dirty well next to the house. I climbed down and cleaned it and laid a new connecting pipe to the house.

One day I asked myself where the sewage flowed to. I discovered the septic tank in a part of the barn by smelling it and with the help of friends pumped the contents out onto the meadow as fertilizer. Afterwards we hosed ourselves clean. Never before had I been in such close contact with my own shit and its stink.

As an architect the source of water and the disposal of sewage should have been clear to me from the beginning. And yet it was not. The knowledge had come from books, was only in my rational mind disconnected from my feelings, my senses and the rest of my body. I had received and stored the information without involving my senses and feelings. According to quantum physics, I had only used a small percentage of my total capacity.

We went on many walks into mountains and forests. The most profound experience was a day we spent in a virgin forest which had not been maintained or interfered with by man for more than 200 years. After having walked alone through the forest for an hour, I felt the urge to take off my clothes and be naked in nature. The act of doing this transported me back into a time when our ancestors lived in forests and had a close and intimate relationship with all its plant and animal life. Shedding my clothes that day was like shedding the layers of civilisation which separated me from my natural environment.

When Bettina became pregnant we prepared for a natural birth either at home or in a hospital which facilitated a natural birth. With the help of books, breathing and a group of pregnant women I became part of the support process to bring the new life into the world. Our daughter was born in a hospital in Germany. Supporting Bettina, holding her during the birthing process, cutting the cord and welcoming our daughter into the world, were the rawest experiences of my life until then.

One day I got a call from a friend of my sister telling me that my sister and her daughter had died in a car accident in Italy. During the period of mourning that followed their deaths, owls came and sat in the trees at night next to our house as if they had come to support and accompany us in our grief.

We could not have lived in this house without the support of our neighbours. On one extremely frosty winter morning when the water pipe was completely frozen, a neighbour came and offered practical help and advice on how to thaw it. When we wanted to get the telephone line brought to our house, another neighbour let us lay the line through his land. When the well dried up after an extended dry period, another neighbour, a member of the voluntary fire brigade, delivered a tank of fresh water and pumped it into our well.

Each morning our closest neighbour would bring us a can of fresh milk before he drove to work.

All of these experiences helped me to become rooted and connected to nature, the surrounding environment and consequently to my own nature. It was the first time in my adult life to experience this deep connection.

Experiences from my childhood on the farm and with the youth group came alive again. My whole being was reawakened by working with my body, getting myself dirty, sweating one season and freezing the next.

A new confidence grew inside me. Living so close to nature taught me that I could survive. These years brought me back to the basics of life: food, shelter, water, birth, death. At times we pushed the boundaries. We fasted, did not read anything for a month or lived for days without a clock. By getting back to basics and connecting to the earth I had come to life again, ready to push the boundaries even further.

Activating my five senses rooted me to the earth. Parallel to that awakening, I also opened my 'inner senses'. We call them vaguely 'the sixth sense'. My experience shows that this 'sixth sense' is not one, but many senses. While the 'outer senses' inform our body, the 'inner senses' inform our soul. Our 'inner senses' sense different levels or frequencies of energy. They include: telepathy, inner navigation, communication with deceased people, contact with higher entities to name just a few. I believe we receive these stimuli from the invisible part of reality through our chakras. I will talk more about them in chapter 5.

We neglect and dismiss our soul in our secular world view and do not nourish our 'inner senses'. Consequently we have to substitute our 'inner senses' with technical devices. Our mobile digital devices help us more and more to communicate with the whole world at any given moment. We can buy things online after seeing an image. Satellite navigation systems direct us to our destination. We can have conference calls with people on the other side of the globe and see each other without travelling. While these devices have many great advantages, they come at a price. I believe that all of these communication and navigation abilities are lying dormant within us. As we become more and more dependent on these technical devices, we risk forgetting that we have these gifts inside us and of losing the trust that they work efficiently.

When we first connect with our inner guiding system to find out what we want and then use the digital devices to support us in achieving our goal, we are giving them their rightful place. When we are connected with our whole body to this earth and centred in our core, we can go into the virtual world and use it to our advantage. Otherwise, we risk getting ever more lost in an endless stream of information.

When we moved from Vienna to the Austrian country side I felt an inner pull to a certain area, without understanding what drew me to an area I had never been before. Following our 'inner guiding system', we found the house within a few days. When we moved to Ireland, it was my 'inner navigation system' which directed me to the place in which we now live. No external device would have brought me to these places. It was my inner guiding system, my inner guide, an inner pull, my soul - whatever name we want to give to it - that directed me. I would not have been able to program a "satnav" system to find it, as I would not have been able to name my destination.

We give priority to our outer senses and are trained today to pick up information from all the different technical devices instead of being able to sense the energy and communicate with the animate, natural world. This is how we have lost our connection with nature. And yet by far the greatest part of our heritage comes from the oral traditions. Our primary forms of communication developed out of the communication with the place, with the genius loci, the spirit of the place.

We isolate ourselves from the knowledge and power available all around us in every moment. We can open up to receive and communicate with higher vibrations of energy, which contain not intellect but intelligence. This intelligence is everywhere, in a stone, a plant, a fellow human being, a place, a house. Everything - literally every thing - is mirroring levels of energy and intelligence which move through us.

Is there something around the house that needs repair and you do not know how to fix it? Get in touch with the specific material. Communicate with it. Ask what needs to be done in order to solve the problem. If a problem arises in your daily life take a walk into nature, ask to communicate with a bush, a flower, a tree. Once you feel drawn to one ask your question and wait for an answer. Humming or rattling will help you to align your energy field to the object you have chosen.

Because our beliefs determine how we perceive the world, our mind tells the eyes what to see, the ears what to hear, the tongue what to taste. I remember telling my sister's partner during one of their visits that he stinks. He challenged me to smell his armpits. To my surprise they smelled fine. It was my belief that he was not supportive of my sister and not the right partner for her that caused my smelling sense to tell me that he stank. My smelling sense had obediently followed the orders of my mind. In the next chapter I will focus on the mind and its belief system.

I will conclude this chapter with a short exercise to bring awareness to your 'outer senses'. I believe that before we can use our 'inner senses' efficiently in our everyday lives, we need to ground ourselves by awakening our five 'outer senses'.

EXERCISE:

There are many ways to activate your 'outer senses'. Become aware of the smells as you pass a bakery or walk into a department store past the perfumes. Go out into nature and smell the rotten leaves in November or the fresh grass in spring. Listen to birds singing or the wind brushing through your hair. Touch a leaf and the bark of a tree. You may want to walk barefoot on grass or wet ground. Enter a children's playground and feel the sand gliding through your fingers or mix earth and water and get your fingers dirty while the gooey, slimy paste brings back memories of early childhood joys. You may want to feel the oil and metal as you repair your car, cycle or motorcycle.

Is there something around the house that needs repair? Get in touch with the specific material. Communicate with it. Ask what needs to be done in order to solve the problem.

If you want a challenge and the opportunity arises, smell and feel fresh cow dung or horse manure. The options are endless once you look for opportunities to awaken your senses.

Choose one exercise a day for the next 3 days.

3. AWARENESS OF BELIEFS

*Most folks are about as happy
as they make up their minds to be.*

Abraham Lincoln

After moving to Ireland I felt a stranger in my new home for many years. On the surface Ireland was a white European society, even though it was called back then the poor house of Europe. Only after moving into our half-finished house and starting to relax, did I allow myself to admit that I felt like an alien. The bog land we had bought was like a wet desert to me. The air was always humid and in constant motion, just like the clouds. The people had a different sense of humour and their thinking seemed to originate from another place, a place unknown to me.

For the first time I became aware of something which I would call 'folk soul', a collective conditioning like a soup in which we all swim. I became only aware that I had dived into a different 'soup' after I had left my homeland and entered a different energy field. I knew I inhabited a different energy field when neighbours asked me how I was and I automatically started to tell them how I felt and what was going on in my life, as I took everything literally. All they expected was an automatic answer, such as "Not too bad" or something similar with the same question tagged on. Prior to moving to Ireland in the mid-80s, we had been caught up in the fear of a nuclear war between the USSR and the US. But people here in Ireland were not concerned with this threat at all. They worried instead about high unemployment and the droves of people emigrating to the US and the UK.

During the difficult settling-in period in County Mayo, we came in contact with the "Option Institute"[8] in Massachusetts. We learned a process with this institute, called the "Option Dialogue Process", which allowed us to question our thoughts and beliefs with an accepting, non-judgemental and loving attitude. During the following years, with the help of thousands of dialogues, I learned to question beliefs which produced my unhappiness. I subsequently became aware of both my personal and collective conditioning in my childhood and the collective conditioning of my new country.

Until then I had neither questioned my beliefs nor their origins. I had automatically soaked them up and acted them out. I never realized that I had chosen them and was free to choose new ones when the old ones did not serve me anymore. Questioning my beliefs was like reorganising and renewing a city. I tore down old buildings (beliefs), built new ones and restructured roads and communication lines which connected different beliefs. I became the architect of my own belief system and I had the freedom to design and choose which beliefs served me and supported my happiness and which ones were outdated and had become destructive.

It was only in hindsight that I could see a relationship between the bog and the questioning of my belief system. The bog in which I lived now and had stirred up with diggers to make drains and a place to build the house, had also stirred up something in me. The bog not only stores butter, corpses and roots of trees for centuries but also memories of past deeds. In my life's story I told about a heap of turf, which belonged to neighbours. Now we learned that these and other neighbours had a right to cut turf on our bog land.

In the following years we eventually solved the legal burdens and at the same time the emotional burdens of hate, revenge, resentment and lack of forgiveness towards people and situations from the past; issues I had brought with me and were now being brought into the light. The resentment and anger of one of the neighbours and his brothers mirrored only my own lack of forgiveness.

I still hated people from my past for what I thought they had done to me, still argued, resented and felt unforgiving. It became clear to me while doing the 'Option Dialogue Process' that they had been doing the best they could to take care of themselves according to their beliefs. Consequently I could see them with love and understanding. I learned that I had only used them to project my unhappiness unto them.

It took me a long time to accept the gifts I had found in Ireland and let go of the past. My new home had different weather, different soil, different seasons, different people and a different culture – a different energy field. Also, living without a car, without newspaper and television supported us in becoming rooted in the place and the building of strong, intimate bonds within the family.

Masaru Emoto, a Japanese scientist, claims that water changes its molecular structure depending on the thoughts and images we have while focusing on the water. That means it contains and stores thoughts. Deciding to live in the wet bog, which acts as a storage for objects, the natural world and also memories, I had indeed chosen the perfect place to become aware and face all the old and often ancient unconscious beliefs which formed my life.

How did I change my beliefs? The questioning process I learned at 'The Option Institute' is simple and unique, yet too complex to be explained in a few sentences. But I will explain it in brief to give you an idea what I mean by questioning my beliefs. The first step is to become aware of unhappy feelings as they arise – anger, sadness, depression, envy, impatience, etc. or destructive behaviour.

According to 'The Option Institute', the cause of the feelings or the behaviour is a belief or set of beliefs that produce this unhappiness. With the help of a mentor, who asks the questions, I first describe the situation or conflict, which has created my unhappiness, thereby clarifying the issue. The question as to why I am unhappy about the situation would then lead to the uncovering of the underlying belief. The mentor then asks why I hold this belief and how does it keeping serve me. I can then decide to change the old belief for one that creates happiness.

Why is a clear mind important when communicating with the energy of a place? Because otherwise my own unresolved issues would cloud my vision. After having connected and communicated with the energy, it is important to translate the images and feelings I have received with a clear, impartial and detached mind. The information can then become concrete, helpful and relevant on a physical level.

If, for example, I hold the belief that invisible energy does not exist, then my senses will tell me that it does not exist.

AWARENESS OF BELIEFS

I will not be willing to tune into it, I will not feel the energy, I will not see images and I will not receive information. Consequently, energy will not exist for me and not be part of my world. Yet, if I am willing to question this belief, new perspectives and aspects may appear which I had not allowed myself to see before.

EXERCISE:

From what you read so far, what judgments do you hold against the content of the book? Write them down. How do you feel, when you hold these judgments? Why do you hold a specific judgment? What are some of the underlying beliefs? How does it serve you to hold these beliefs? If you have negative feelings around these beliefs, turn the beliefs around by changing them into positive beliefs. Find reasons why a specific new view would serve you better. How do you feel now? Do you still want to hold on to your original view?

4. AWAKENING THE SOUL

*All that you behold, though it appears Without,
It is Within,
in your Imagination,
of which this World of Mortality is but a shadow.*

William Blake

*Logic will bring you from A to B.
Imagination will take you everywhere.*

Albert Einstein

During the process of questioning our beliefs we had decided to home-school our children. We taught them right through primary school and most of secondary school. I felt that the mainstream school curriculum focused on their rational mind too early, and prohibited the development of their intuitive side. Painting, singing, playing, writing, inventing stories, learning the alphabet by connecting each letter to a fairy tale, learning the mathematical tables by singing them, being out in nature, reading to them most days after lunch created a connection between us and fostered the development of our intuitive, creative and emotional side of the brain.

More than anything else my children taught me that connection is based on a willingness to let go of expectations, limitations and the will to be right. They taught me over and over again that my belief, that I am the one who knows right from wrong, does not result in an open and happy relationship. In order to connect with a place, a house, an environment, other people and other cultures and to widen our perspective of how we perceive ourselves and the world, we must be willing to let go of expectations and a certain outcome.

I am sharing my experience of home-schooling with you because in hindsight I realize that it has helped me to deepen my connection to the right side of the brain.

I want to elaborate a bit further here on the importance of developing the right side of our brain. We in the western world put more and more emphasis on the left side of the brain. Without being aware of it, we pay a high price for this imbalance as I will show in the following investigation of the processes within our brain. I decided to elaborate on this topic as it provides an essential key to understanding the connection between the energy within us and the energy in the surrounding environment.

We have two sides of the brain. The right side is intuitive, creative, imaginative, general, conceptual, emphatic and irregular, and only perceives the whole. Its language consists of images, symbols, vibrations, colours and feelings. It has no concept of past or future, of here and there. It answers a question with "maybe so, maybe not".

The left side is rational, logical, analytical, precise, repetitive, detached, literal and factual, and organises information in a linear, detailed, structured way. Its language is made of words and numbers. It answers with a definite "yes or no".

These two sides represent the masculine and the feminine, black and white, day and night, life and death and the endless variations of duality inherent to our world.

In my understanding language originally arose out of energy fields of stretches of land. This is why still, even today, different regions have their particular accent. And this is why names of places often reflect the energy of the place. It was only rather recently that with the formation of nation states language was standardised. So today there are rules that determine the standard use of English or American English, German, Austrian or Swiss German. I know this is much more complex. My main point is that language and culture were closely related to the land and that people intuitively picked up the energetic quality of places as we often can see in the names of places.

In order to explain the different functions of the right and left hemisphere of the brain, I include here parts of a talk given by Jill Bolte Taylor, Ph. D., a neuron anatomist at Harvard University entitled: "How it feels to have a stroke"[9].

In this talk, Taylor explains what happened when a blood vessel suddenly ruptured in the left half of her brain and how she could no longer process information as a result. Four hours after the rupture she could neither walk nor talk, read nor write, or recall any part of her life. She became an infant in a grown up body. The experience with just the right side of her brain working, allowed her to get to know its properties.

Taylor says: "The right side is about the present moment (...) the here and now, thinks in pictures and learns (...)

through the movement of our bodies. Information in the form of energy streams in simultaneously through all our senses (...). I am an energy being connected to the energy all around me through the consciousness of the right hemisphere."

"Our left hemisphere is a very different place. It thinks linearly and methodically. Our left hemisphere is all about the past and all about the future (...). (It) takes out of this enormous collage (of information) details and more details about these details. It then organises and categorises all this information and associates with everything we ever learned in the past and projects it into the future (...). Our left hemisphere thinks in language (...). It reminds me when I have to do my laundry, but probably most importantly when this little voice says 'I am' and as soon as my left hemisphere says 'I am', I become a separate being from the energy flow around me."

After she had had this stroke, she could not see her body in the normal way. "I could no longer define the boundaries of my body, (...) define where I begin and where I end, because the atoms and molecules of my arm blended with the atoms and molecules of the wall and all I could detect was this energy."

"There was no mind chatter, (...) (but) total silence. I felt enormous and expansive. I felt at one with all the energy and it was beautiful there."

Jill Bolte Taylor's description above gives a wonderful illustration of how the two hemispheres of the brain receive and process information differently and how each hemisphere has its own language.

When we enter a new space or meet a person for the first time, we sense their essential quality in the first few seconds. In these first few moments the right side of the brain processes the information and gives us a whole image of the space or the person. Then the rational mind asks, whether this is good or bad for me. Based on past experiences the rational mind makes a judgment. If the answer is no, this is bad for me, then the old reptilian part of the brain sees three options: fight, freeze or flight. This is our normal mechanical, automatic and reactive behavioural pattern.

When we want to connect to higher frequencies of energy we have to stay in contact with the right side of the brain, be curious, investigate, communicate, ask questions, feel our way into the images received, dive into the unknown, move with the flow and trust the process as it unfolds.

When we judge, have expectations or are attached to the outcome, we know that we have chosen our rational mind as the source of information. We are no longer connected and in an isolated bubble instead. When we feel, we open the gate to the intuitive mind, but when we think, we disconnect from the whole and focus on details only.

As I mentioned before: I was 18 months old, when I was suddenly paralysed and clinically dead for a short period of time. My mother, for her own reasons, was not connected to her soul. I had tried to connect to her with the rational mind at a far too early stage. At the same time it was "mission impossible" trying to connect with the rational mind as it is the very nature of the rational mind to perceive details and fragments. For me as an infant being disconnected from my mother was like being cut off from the life forces that were there to sustain me and allowed me to grow.

We know from research in neurology that the right side of the brain develops first in an infant and later begins to inform the left side of the brain. The intuitive side calls for connection and communication. This is her nature and essence. It learns through play and movement. When this soul connection is interrupted, it has, based on my own experience, severe consequences for the child's survival or at least its natural healthy growth. My own experiences include: developing a stutter, becoming extremely shy and having the feeling for most of my life of not belonging, of being an alien in this world.

It becomes clear from Jill Bolte Taylor's experience that we need both sides of the brain and the connection between the two in order to function and survive in this world, but more importantly to live a creative, inspired, happy and fulfilled life. From an anatomical perspective, it is the corpus callosum, a string of nerve fibres which connects the two hemispheres of the brain. When both sides of the brain are connected the answer is not anymore 'yes' or 'no' or 'maybe so, maybe not', but a resounding 'yes, yes'.

We, as Taylor's experience and explanations make clear, could not live in this physical world with only the right side of the brain receiving and processing information. The important question is, which side is dominant and which side is subordinate? Is it the left side, which only sees separate details or is it the right side which perceives an ever changing multidimensional reality and can therefore see the whole picture? When we feel and connect with the energy first, the left side can then tune into the details and organise life on the physical plane.

Albert Einstein, the great physicist, describes very well what has happened in the world today: 'The intuitive mind is a sacred gift and the rational mind is a faithful servant.

We have created a society that honours the servant and has forgotten the gift'.

I also think of the story of the group of blind men, who define an elephant by touching different parts of his body: One by touching his ear lobe, the other his trunk, a third his hind leg and so on. Each one wants to define the whole elephant by getting to know only a certain specific part of his body and each one thinks he is right.

So what is it that hinders us from allowing the right hemisphere of the brain, our soul, the part in us that perceives the whole, to lead our life? What is it in you? When I answer it for myself it is the fear of not being able to physically survive in this world, earn money, the fear of not belonging to the community, the fear of being nobody, the fear of standing alone, the fear of going into the unknown. Fear, fear, fear. It is fear that holds me back, fear of the separated, individual "I" when I choose to identify with I the architect, husband, father, born in Vienna, now stranger in Ireland. There is nothing wrong with playing these roles as long as I do not identify with them.

How can my fractured, detail-focused, individual self know what's best for me? When I tune into the right side of the brain, I get a whole image, but I am unable to function in this physical reality. I therefore get the whole picture from the right side of the brain first, then translate it and bring it in context with the specific task with the help of the logical mind. In this way each side does what it does best and a connecting bridge is created through their collaboration. Once again it is all about connection; the connection between the left and right hemisphere and the fact that each side takes its rightful place.

From my personal experience I see the brain as a receiver and processor of information. It is not the source just like a television set is not the source of the images we see and the words we hear. Children may believe that the people we see on the screen are in the box. And yet most adults in Western society would believe that we are the source of our thoughts, when all we are mere receivers, processors and transmitters of information. We can, however, decide on the source of our information and what information we take in by choosing the channel we tune into.

When the television set stops working or is turned off, all the channels are still transmitting their programs. Similarly, if we are not able to tune into the energy of a place, it does not mean the energy does not exist. We have simply chosen not to tune into it. After we die, our bodies cannot receive, process and transmit information anymore. But all the information is still being broadcast and the consciousness which chose the programs is still alive.

When I connect with the spirit of a place, I set an intention to get in contact with that spirit. I consequently connect and get what I was asking for. When we are not focused we are open to any sort of random information.

I remember the inner chaos, uncertainty and confusion I felt as a student of architecture, when I was given a fictional site map to design a house. I did not know the actual site, the neighbouring environment or the clients. I saw thousands of possibilities, but had nothing that grounded me or connected me to the energetic reality of a specific place with a specific client. How could I have not felt confused? No wonder we so often experience modern architecture as being soulless.

This chapter is focused on soul. So, what do I mean by soul? Soul is a word which is not much in fashion these days. For many years I was confused about the meaning of soul. When I research on the internet and go to Wikipedia, I find statements like the following: The soul (...) is the incorporeal and (...) immortal essence of a person, living thing or object. Soul can function as a synonym for spirit, mind, psyche or self. Aristotle called soul psyche: psyche meaning life, spirit, consciousness. It refers also to the vital breath. In Latin soul means anima. We use the word when we say something or someone is animated, meaning alive; as is an animal. For Kant soul is the "I", an inner experience which can neither be proved nor disproved (...).

To make things more confusing, the term "psychology" literally means "study of the soul". But contemporary psychology is defined as the study of mental processes and behaviour (en.wikipedia.org). The more I continue reading about the meaning of soul, the more confused I get.

For me soul refers to the mysterious, the invisible, the empty space, the essential quality, the core energy. My understanding is that, dependent on the development of our soul, soul means something different for each of us.

As I will explore in the next chapter, there are different frequencies or levels of energy. Depending on the level of our energy field - or aura or consciousness - soul has a different meaning. And then all the different meanings are right based on the level of a person's consciousness.

I believe that we are born into this life with a specific purpose. As we grow we encounter conflicts between the world's goals and our soul's purpose or vision. In order to survive and adapt we split off parts of our soul. In this process we become more and more separated from the earth, our bodies, our feelings and from who we really are. In this way we accumulate undigested life experiences which show up in both physical and psychological illness and all kinds of unhappiness.

The deeds created out of this separation manifest also in the spaces and places we inhabit. By clearing the energy in these places and spaces we also purify and liberate parts of our soul. Do we dare meet our shadows and start to digest the experiences we split off or freeze?

The other day I noticed my laptop running slower. A friend came and ran a program called a de-fragmentation process. I watched a graphic with hundreds of squares, mostly red, a few blue, some starting to flicker orange and turn green. The task of the program was to put things back into their proper place. When we work on something, then drop it somewhere and start the next work, over time our desk, our house or our workshop becomes so clattered, it takes ages to find things. When we leave conflicts with our partner, family or neighbour unresolved, the flow of communication will slow down, until we have nothing to say to each other.

When our soul is scattered into thousand pieces as each shock and traumatic experience fragments it more, the sense of loss and exhaustion reaches a point of crisis, which eventually forces us to pay attention:

To focus on our soul,
to bring order back into our life,
to align the fragmented pieces,
bring the herd home and
feel the pain of loss.
This is the night of the soul,
the acknowledgment of our unhappiness,

time to look within
and accept our shadows
instead of blaming everyone and everything
for providing a mirror of our shame.
When you watch this process of de-fragmentation
of your hardware, you may get a sense
of the patience, perseverance and faith it takes
to bring every part back into its rightful place.
It does not happen automatically.
We can't leave, knowing that the program
will do its work and busy ourselves with other things.
We need to do the work,
seemingly endless, sometimes hopeless,
always leading to a happier, more peaceful, successful life
filled with ease and joy.

Connecting and collaborating with the place we inhabit is one of the ways to reconnect to our soul. Whatever we encounter in life offers the choice of either connection or separation. What is it you pay attention to? What do you love to do with your whole heart and soul?

EXERCISE:

You are most likely fortunate enough to feed your body more than once a day. How often do you feed your soul? Do you write a journal, play an instrument, listen with total attention to your partner or children, go out into nature, sing or dance on a regular basis? Do you have a meditation practice? In other words, how do you nourish your soul?

Choose one of the above activities and do it once a day for 7 days and then reflect on possible benefits for your life.

In case you nourish your soul on a regular basis, do you know the name of your soul? Spiritual teachers sometimes give their students a name which relates to their soul. If you do not know the name of your soul I suggest that you ask its name and communicate with it about the meaning of this name. The name may give you insights into your essence and purpose in this life.

5. RAISING THE FREQUENCY OF OUR ENERGY FIELD

*We can't solve problems by using
the same kind of thinking
we used when we created them.*

Albert Einstein

Even after many dialogues investigating my thinking I was still compulsively controlling and angry at times if things didn't go my way. I was very aware of my beliefs, yet very slow to change them. I still carried a lot of guilt and anger within me.

After taking part in an eight week program, entitled 'Living the Dream' at "The Option Institute", a shift happened and from that point onwards my life and my perception of myself and the world changed for the better.

Looking back I believe that the frequency of my energy field increased after this shift. The higher vibrations allowed transformations which were not possible before. I believe it was the higher frequency of energy of the teacher and the place which triggered my own potential and liberated the higher frequencies in me.

RAISING THE FREQUENCY OF OUR ENERGY FIELD

Up until now I have talked about the importance of opening our senses, of clearing our minds of negative emotions, of giving precedence to the right side of the brain, which perceives wholeness, and thereby allowing the rational mind do what it does best: focus on details. For this shift to happen, we need higher energy frequencies. These frequencies will also enable us to tune into the energies of places, transform these energies and allow the essence of a place to support us.

I said on several occasions before that my intention is to communicate with the essence of a place. With essence I mean the blue print or matrix, which like a seed contains the whole building plan and purpose of the place. An acorn contains the blue print of an oak. Within each of us there is an energetic core that contains our life's purpose.

Imagine an apple cut in two parts horizontally. There are seeds around the core, but the very centre is empty space. It represents the essence of the apple: the potential to grow into an apple tree with its roots, branches, flowers and fruits. It is the invisible chi, prana, life force, which enables the tree to grow into its specific shape. This core energy informs the seeds. This is how the apple tree fulfils its purpose.

We can only feel into this essence, an energy field without images, colours, symbols, words or numbers. When I get in contact with the essence, I often laugh involuntarily. I feel this essence within my heart, not my physical heart, but what we call the core or centre of our being. Once we feel into the essential quality of a space or place, it can then be translated or transformed into images and colours, words and numbers and eventually into material reality.

I compare this process of transformation from higher frequency to a dense, lower frequency with the use of power lines. A 400,000 Volt electricity line needs transformers to transform it to 220 or 110 Volt. The power can now be used in everyday life. Our energy body can, when trained, also work as an energy transformer.

These energetic transformations are at the core of my work with a place. For this process of transformation we need to bring 'light from above to places of darkness', higher frequencies to places of lower, denser frequency. We need to bring energy, blocked because of misuse of energy in the past, back into a flow.

To get a better and broader understanding of the different levels of energy and the different frequencies, I will outline briefly three different models of energy. The first model refers to our chakras, which are energy points in the body that receive and radiate energy, which I like to see as our 'inner senses'. They could also be described as dynamic vortices of subtle energies.

When we open our chakras, our 'inner senses', we can access the energy fields in and around us. Marko Pogacnic[10] shows us in the second model the different levels of energy in and around the Earth.

Consequently we have the potential to transform different levels of energy. The third model by J.G.Bennett[11], an English physicist and student of the spiritual teacher Gurdjieff, focuses on the transformation of us humans.

As most of us are used to living in a one dimensional reality, i.e. a material world view, the following description of the existence of a multidimensional reality may seem strange, but it can help to broaden our perspective and comprehend that the split rational mind has no means of perceiving such a reality.

I have learned from experience that our own transformation is the prerequisite to communicating and cooperating with the Earth. However, understanding the different frequencies or levels of energy can help us in our own personal transformation.

1. The seven energy chakras

I start with describing a well known model from the Eastern traditions: our seven energy chakras or seven doorways through which universal energy enters our body. Our chakras are spinning vortices, vibrating and pulsating disks, which draw in energy of a certain frequency. In chapter 2 I suggested that these chakras are our 'inner senses'. These seven energy wheels are individually known as the root chakra, sacral chakra, solar plexus, heart chakra, throat chakra, 3rd eye chakra and crown chakra.

When all our chakras are open, we can receive all levels and frequencies of energy and live from a perspective of wholeness. When the energy in one of the chakras is weak, we see it reflected in problems in our life. So, for example, will strong energy in the heart chakra be reflected in strong and loving relationships, or a weak throat chakra will indicate an issue with speaking our truth and being authentic.

Just as our body has points where energy is drawn in, so has the earth[12]. These earth chakras are in different places on the earth. Each one has a specific function. At the same time they are connected with each other.

2. Model by Marko Pogacnik

The second model shows the different levels of earth's energy frequencies, starting with the densest. It was developed by the German physicist Burkhard Heim and is adapted by the geomancer Marco Pogacnik in his book *Synchrone Welten, Geomantie des zwoelfdimensionalen Lebensraums (Synchronic Worlds, Geomancy of the twelve-dimensional realm)*.

The first dimension is a point, the second a line and third is space. The fourth dimension is time. In the following I will go more into detail with the fifth to eighth dimension as they are most relevant to our topic.

Fifth Dimension: Biosphere

The fifth dimension is called Biosphere. It can be vaguely compared with the vital energy in Bennett's model below. The Biosphere contains the life forces that move the blood in our body, get our digestive system working and our lungs breathing and the heart pumping. It is the flow of energy from the roots of plants through the stem to the leaves and blossoms and fruits. Life on a physical plain would not be possible without this energy.

Physical outdoor activity and a healthy diet, which contains a lot of life force as in biologically grown food, can increase our level of life force. Junk food and drugs, such as alcohol and nicotine, reduce it. Western medicine looks at the symptoms of sickness in the physical body and fights them. Eastern medicine, like Aryuveda in India or Acupuncture from China, focuses on restoring health by increasing the life force in the body.

In relation to places and buildings we look out for signs in nature and in the building which may indicate that something is out of balance or indeed its beauty awakens a sense of peace and freedom in us. When the energy is flowing we will feel its aliveness and it will show in the abundance of the natural environment. Damp walls and/or mould on the walls or a warped timber floor are warning signs of a deeper conflict.

Sixth Dimension: Noosphere

The sixth dimension is the dimension of consciousness, which he calls Noosphere. It contains the evolutionary process from a local, tribal consciousness to a national, global and ultimately universal consciousness. This is where we form identity. At this level we can raise awareness of our conditioning. This is the level of the personality of a place and where we can become aware of energy blocks. In order to release these energy blocks in us and in our environment, we have to access higher levels of energy.

In order to get in contact with these higher dimensions, we have to use the sixth dimension as a doorway. This can be the biggest stumbling block. So let's look closer at this sixth dimension.

The consciousness of the earth is one of duality. It is therefore important to live in this creative tension of right and wrong, good and bad, light and dark, day and night. I have focused on one aspect in the previous chapter in connection with the left side and the right side of the brain. With the dawn of the Age of Enlightenment we dismissed the information received by the right side of the brain. The servant has subsequently become the master as we subordinated the gift of intuition to logic, as Einstein remarked. The more our lives are guided by the rational mind, the more we become separated from ourselves, our environment, the earth as a living entity and the universe. We become more and more cut off from higher levels of energy.

In order to correct this imbalance, we have to reawaken the right side of the brain. We have to feel our pain, our anger, our sadness, our frustration, so that feelings of joy and gratitude can emerge. We relearn the language of the universe, which is accessed through feeling and not through thinking. The imaginative, intuitive side can again become the master and the rational mind its useful servant. Now real intelligence from a perspective of wholeness can emerge.

If we don't heal this pain of separation it can lead to addictions in all its forms, such as alcohol and drugs to sex and work, consumerism and food to soothe the underlying pain and sense of loss. The German language reflects the connection between search and addiction. 'Suche' means search and has the same root as 'Sucht' meaning addiction. The list of ways in which we try to fill this hole is endless. Western societies are starting to become aware that this way of living is unsustainable, but we are still unaware that it is caused by our sense of separation. We subsequently continue to pollute ourselves, our food, our environment and, more importantly, our thoughts and feelings.

When Bettina and I first have seen the place in which we now live on an unusually hazy day, I felt a vibrancy in the contrast between the blue, moving water of the lake and the brown harshness of the bog. It was only during the next visit that I saw the wide, expansive views all around and felt at the same time a motherly, sheltering and embracing quality in the place. Exposed yet embracing, wide open skies above and the black bog below, water from the lake and wind blowing on top of a hill, light and dark, masculine and feminine, opposites always calling for union. I was attracted by this duality which mirrored our own energy field as a couple at the time.

But it was the flash of light I saw over the lake for a moment as we viewed the place for the first time that let me decide to settle here. Today I see it as a sign of hope that there was also a unifying energy on the place that would support us in transforming our duality into union. This would be energy of the eighth dimension and I will talk more about it a bit further below.

Seventh Dimension: Earth Cluster

The seventh dimension of even higher frequency brings us in contact with what Pogacnic calls the Earth Cluster. Apart from the material earth sphere, he also identifies other spheres or parallel worlds not seen by our physical eyes. They are close to or within the material world. There is a primordial fairy world that sustains the natural world. Then there is a world of ancestors and descendants were souls rest between incarnations and further more a "book of life" which contains the matrix for our time-space everyday world. Within the earth there are layers of past civilisations, such as Atlantis - where the whole globe was covered in water - and Lemuria - when the planet had cooled down sufficiently but still had a fiery quality to it - and a future civilisation he calls Krex, which will be based on the element of air.

In this seventh dimension we can therefore tune into souls of deceased people, into past civilisations and historic moments which left scars in the earth's energy field. Here we can get into contact with extra-terrestrial beings and with nature spirits such as gnomes, fairies and leprechauns. The "book of life" is also here, where psychics tune in to tell us about past life experiences and to predict our future.

If we have not dealt with our own past and the issues we may have taken on from past generations, we will not be able to get in contact with this level in the world at large. The deeper we get to know ourselves, the more we will become conscious of these invisible layers all around us. As a consequence of this awareness and clearing past issues we feel connected to and an integral part of both the earth and the universe.

Tuning into this dimension in places and spaces, gives us insights into a wide variety of forms and images. We might become aware of a previous battle field through the presence of souls who are still frozen in shock. Or we may encounter dampness in walls, which has its cause in angry souls not willing to forgive their relatives for casting them out of the family unit (see Chapter 8 below regarding a place in Connemara, County Galway, Ireland).

In the place Bettina and I live, we encountered burdens and cleared the crime of a forged signature. Only after souls from famine times were released of their suffering, were we free to open our home and share it through gatherings and workshops with other people in the wider community. But it needed higher frequencies of energy to release these energy blocks. While doing this process on our home, I went back three generations into my own family's past and became aware of unresolved issues which I had unconsciously carried as my own.

Eighth Dimension: Causal Body

Only in the eighth dimension, the causal body, can the cause of all the dramas and energy blocks be released. We can align the energy here and restore harmony. By being in contact with the eighth dimension, we are able to remember the purpose of our life. This is the blue print or matrix for our life. There are also places, which are connected to higher universal energy and their purpose is to serve the greater well-being of all life on earth. It is therefore of great importance that these universal energies can flow freely and any old issues are cleared. Access to the higher levels of the eighth and ninth dimension is necessary to enable the cosmic energy to heal and liberate the spirit of a place.

3. Model by J.G.Bennett

I introduce his concept and ideas about energy, which are, even though they are 50 years old, still new and unconventional. His ideas may broaden our understanding and view of the world and life as we understand it.

When I read Bennett's book for the first time 35 years ago, I was totally blown away. It was the beginning of my exploration of energies within my being and in relation to others and the earth.

In his book, *Energies: Material, Vital, Cosmic*, he explains energy as follows:

"In the ordinary school teaching of mechanics, energy is defined as the power to do work. Here only mechanical work is referred to, but the same definition can be applied to energies that have nothing to do with ordinary mechanics. Whatever kind of work we have to do, we need the corresponding or right kind of energy. For example, if I want my watch to go, I have to wind up the spring (...). If I want to cook an egg, I have to boil water – but it is of no use putting my watch on the gas stove to get it wound up (...). It is just the same with our psychic functions. Each kind of inner work requires energy of a particular quality".

He divides energies into 3 categories and 12 qualities or levels of energy:

MECHANICAL ENERGY

12 Dispersed Energy
11 Directed Energy
10 Cohesive Energy
9 Plastic Energy

The Mechanical Energy group has the lowest frequency and within that heat (Dispersed Energy) is the lowest form of energy, passive, chaotic and disorganised. The level above that, Directed Energy, is present in the motion of a train, gravitation and magnetism. The next level (Cohesive Energy) contains all solid bodies and liquids and has cohesive or chemical energy. And the last category in the group of Mechanical Energies, (Plastic Energy) is used by our bodies to move and change shape without falling apart.

LIFE ENERGIES

    8   Constructive Energy
    7   Vital Energy
    6   Automatic Energy
    5   Sensitive Energy

Bennett calls the next group of higher frequency energies, Life Energies. The first category is Constructive Energy, which has the power to organise and produce patterns. We find it in our DNA and the workings of enzymes and hormones. One level above this is Vital Energy, which gets our blood flowing and our nerves energized. When our body dies, this energy is set free and available to other forms of life. He calls the next form of energy, Automatic Energy. We behave as if we were free, but inside we work like a machine and do not perceive any choice in the way we think, feel and behave. This is the level of our separate ego identity, our personality. The last of the life energies are Sensitive Energies, which become active in us as soon as we become aware of our behaviour, feelings and thoughts (our bodies, senses and mind). On this level we experience ourselves as the observer and the observed.

COSMIC ENERGIES

    4   Conscious Energy
    3   Creative Energy
    2   Unitive Energy
    1   Transcendent Energy

Bennett calls the highest group of energies Cosmic Energies, as they come from beyond our earthly, embodied, sensual experience. The first is Consciousness, which is both in us and beyond our limited ego identity, connecting us to something greater than our selves. The next higher level he calls Creative Energy, which creates works of art and inventions in science. It is what we might call inspiration or spontaneity. The two highest levels of energy cannot be experienced directly or only in flashes. Unitive Energy is understood as the energy that integrates and makes whole. Bennett refers to the highest energy, which "we can neither know its action nor know how it is organised in the universe" (pg. 17) as Transcendent Energy, the creative source of the universe.

To make the above more concrete, I want to give two examples. It happens quite often that when I speak in front of or with people, I start to cry. My understanding is that a higher frequency of energy wants to move through me. The words which want to be spoken are coming from a higher level – from Creative or Unitive Energy – and my ego first needs to be broken open and the vessel widened in order for the energy and its intelligence and power to be expressed.

The breaking open would then be the Sensitive Energy. This state of vulnerability is for me the doorway into Universal Energies. When I allow myself to cry in front of other people, the crying becomes laughter and with the laughter comes power and clarity, creativity and compassion. With my decision to allow myself to be vulnerable I have stepped through the doorway. I have made a conscious decision (consciousness level) to behave against my conditioning that it is inappropriate for a man to cry in public, which is the level of Automatic Energy. Only now can I express creative thought with power and conviction.

Another example is the changing of beliefs. When I first become aware that I am unhappy, I am using Sensitive

Energy. I am willing to ask myself about the cause of my unhappiness, which comes from the level of consciousness. Now Creative Energy can come in and help me see the situation from a wider perspective and I can choose a new belief, which gives me feelings of happiness and joy. I see that the old belief, which comes from the level of Automatic Energy, does not serve me anymore.

As the earth is not separate from the rest of the universe these Cosmic Energies are also within and around the earth. In this way the earth is in communication with the universe. Once we open ourselves to the different energy levels within us, we can tune into all living things, be them rocks, animals, plants or fellow human beings, and all beings invisible to us. We become active participants in a universal process.

If I encounter blocked energy in a place, I need an awareness of this block, a consciousness and a will that it will be transformed. Creative energy can then dissolve the block and allow the energy to flow again. If these higher levels of frequency are not available to me, then I may be aware of a block or I may perceive it as a problem. But I can't do anything about it.

I want to stress here that we need to ask for permission in the process of communication. It may well be that either we or the energetic entity of the place is not yet ready for a transformation or change.

In order to get to the cause of the problem, I have to let go of my small limited self. By letting go of any solutions, judgments, attachments or expectations the ego may have, the higher vibrations of energy can flow through me. Only then can the intelligence and the power of the higher energy frequency dissolve what the ego has perceived as a problem.

When I feel the energy of the place, the place and I become one and this alignment is the healing. When we no longer feel separate from our surroundings, we experience an increasing connection with both the universe and the inner earth. This connection will manifest in a more loving relationship with ourselves as well as in an abundant and happy life.

You may feel confused after reading about three different models of energy. This is quite a normal response as the mind's inner order is greatly disturbed when a lot of new information is received. We remain confused until we have accepted and integrated the new information. Alternatively, we can shut down and reject the new ideas.

My aim in presenting these ideas is only to tickle and broaden your mind and not to press my experiences into any model or box. I certainly do not want to intellectualize it. My sole aim here is for your mind to become more flexible and for your heart to open.

The image of a radio comes to mind in regard to the tuning into the different frequencies of energy. By changing the frequency, we get access to different radio stations and their programs. We can tune into different frequencies and receive different 'programs' and messages. What are the stations or energy fields we can tune into?

We can tune into nature spirits, into the souls of deceased people, into the past and into the future, into past civilisations, into aliens, into the spiritual light network spanning the globe like an international electricity network, into the communication networks of nature spirits, into the specific personality of a place, an area and its purpose – to mention but a few.

In our culture we only acknowledge energies from the vital energies downwards and can therefore only acknowledge what we can see and touch as real. Reality is out there. We strive to get everything we need from the external reality.

To get in contact with the energies of places and spaces is an inner experience. And even though the cosmic or universal energies are objective, they become subjective as they are filtered through our personal beliefs.

As I said, I am introducing these ideas only to tickle the mind. And if you are interested to learn more about it, I highly recommend that you read Bennett's book mentioned above. But as long as we don't feel these energies within us, as long as we don't use these higher levels of energy to transform blocked energies in our bodies, loosen our old concepts to receive new ideas, let emotions of grief and anger sweep through us, we are still operating from our mind. We may understand and accept these new ideas with our mind, but until we actually feel the energy and the power and intelligence of the energy, we are still unable to communicate with this vast intelligence all around us.

Therefore, I can't stress this often enough that we must first do our own inner transformation, which starts with the questions, "Who am I?" and "What is my purpose in this life?" Once we have found answers to these questions and start living the answers, it becomes natural to communicate with various aspects of invisible worlds. Even though Beethoven was deaf, he could compose music he heard with his inner ear. The Moken tribe off the coast of Thailand recognized the signs of the approaching tsunami both in the water and in animal behaviour on December 2004.

They all fled to high ground and survived the tsunami, while their villages and boats were destroyed. The more we get in contact with ourselves, the more the inner and the outer worlds become one. Whatever I am in contact with within myself, is mirrored outside in the external physical world.

In the 16th century we discovered our planet from pole to pole by travels on water and on land. Today we can zoom in with the help of Google Earth into every part of the world. A satellite can spy the lightning of a cigarette on earth. We have set foot on the moon and send space ships to the edges of our solar system. The new paradigm calls for a new journey of discovery and this time we are called to go within. Only by getting to know our inner selves, are we able to feel higher levels of energy. As Bennett points out all the energies, starting from vital energy and moving upwards, can only be experienced from the inside.

We can receive support from the earth and in turn support and help the earth and other beings. When energy can flow freely through us, it can also flow freely around us. Inside and outside merge into one field of energy. The place and space we live in supports us on different levels and we in turn feel at home and happy and support the free flow of energy around us.

I experience the Celtic Cross as a symbol of this inner transformation process. The horizontal line represents the right and left side of the brain. The right side becomes the master and the left side its servant. The vertical line represents the light from above and the darkness from below. In our brain the lowest is the old reptilian brain. Its task is to survive, fight for its territory and seek dominance and power. It is overlaid by the mammalian brain, which has feelings such as attachment, anger and fear but also cares. The human brain is the last in our evolution. With the help of universal energies we are able to transform lower thinking, feeling and behaving into higher frequencies. In this way we lay open our core, which is shown in the circle of the Celtic cross.

When we go deep enough into darkness we come to the core of the earth which is light energy, the Spirit of the Earth, Gaia. As it is above, so it is below. Both transformation processes, horizontal and vertical, set free a centre, a core, an essence. It was always present, only hidden and forgotten. This core energy contains consciousness, intelligence, power, creativity and a connecting force we call love; energies J.G.Bennett calls universal energies.

EXERCISE:

In order to connect to the energy field within you and around you sit down or lie down and breathe. You can do the exercise either in your home or preferably in nature. Fill first your pelvic bowl and then up to your chest with breath. The in-breath takes effort, the out-breath is a letting go. Imagine a wave building up and then crashing. Your mouth is open. The breath is connected, meaning there is no pause between in-breath and out-breath. Do you feel the energy moving? Are you aware of areas where energy is blocked? Are the inner and outer energy fields merging? Do the exercise for 15-30 minutes for at least 3 days.

PART II
PLACES AND SPACES

*Nothing so blinding as perception of form.
For sight of form means understanding
has been obscured.*

A Course in Miracles, Text

Last night we watched the film Pina Bausch, *Dance, dance, less we all die* about the dancer and teacher Pina Bausch and her group. The film started with the question, "How do we express ourselves in situations where we are speechless and allow the body to speak?" We saw fascinating bodies leaping, falling, catching, diving, grieving or celebrating. These bodies were being moved effortlessly by energy without any interference from the conditioned mind.

How does this relate to the subject of this book? The ultimate goal of energy work is to allow energy flow freely, whether in a human or a place or a building. The dancers expressed feelings and situations through dance using facial expression and body language. This is a universal language that enables us to communicate independently of culture, creed or ethnicity.

In this second part of my book I will demonstrate with examples how a free flow of energy can be restored by tuning into the energy of places and spaces. These examples will show that it is through a conscious decision that we connect and communicate with our environment.

By now we have opened up to the idea of tuning into invisible realities with the help of our inner senses. How we integrate our experiences with different levels of energy depends, I believe, on our level of consciousness.

One way of looking at it is to see that I am the observer and the place or building is being observed. As I get in contact with the energy of the building or place, something new is formed. A third force comes into being as the perceived separation between subject and object dissolves. A new relational space or energy field develops out of this connection. It is this relational space which contains the information and power I receive and feel.

Buckminster Fuller, an American architect, system theorist, author, designer and inventor said: "There is no universal space or static space in the universe. We have relationships – not space." What holds the whole universe together and keeps it in motion is this relationship between the stars, suns and galaxies. This relationship brings the building in which we live to life and creates the sense of home for us.

Another way of understanding this concept is that there is really no world out there. The world I perceive is simply a mirror of my inner state of mind. We really make it all up. From the millions of stimuli we receive every moment, we pick up a limited amount, choose to make them into certain images which make sense to us and thus give meaning to the world we perceive. This explains why everyone receives different images when one gets in contact with the energy of a place. And yet the core of the energy beyond words and images is the same.

I remember meeting a Shaman from northern Mexico who told us about going on a vision quest once a year to communicate with the sun. Someone coming from a Christian background might see an image of the Son of God, a Buddhist might see Buddha and someone else might see light. The images may differ, depending on our cultural programming, but the essence is the same.

So how do we get in contact with these energies, feel into a place and receive information, power and transformation? How does this process of communicating with the energy of a place actually work? (You will need to adapt the suggestions depending on whether you are already living in a particular space or considering buying or renting.)

Below I will describe seven rules or steps for working with energy which crystallized for me over time. Before that, I would like to share three overriding principles about the energies of places. They are either on a personality level or on a higher energy frequency. It is the same as with us humans. We either have a personal, mainly private life, or the main focus of our life is to serve society in a political, educational, economic, religious, entertaining etc. role. When we enter the energy field of a place or building, we do not yet know the quality of energy we will be getting in contact with.

Additional to these two principles, a place or space can have its energies blocked. In order to get support from the spirit of the place, we first need to bring the energy back into flow. Therefore it is important to keep in mind that we are faced with a number of unknown factors beyond the scope of the rational mind.

The 7 steps of connection with the spirit of a place

1. *We need to acknowledge that we do not know. Each place is different, so the experience of connection is also different. Therefore we go to the place, site or house with an open mind, with no agenda with regard to the experience or the outcome.*

2. *Walk around. Keep your gaze relaxed and your outer and inner senses open. Notice the vegetation. Are there obstacles like densely grown bushes along the entrance road which almost block your way to the house? Is the vegetation lush and abundant, or does it feel weak or neglected? Is there rubbish on the site? How do you feel, when you enter the space? Do your feelings change? Is the house full of clutter?*

3. *After these first impressions ask questions about the history of the house or place. What attracts you to the place? Where do you perceive a problem? Are you uncomfortable around something? Listen carefully to the answers, without judging or drawing any conclusions. Consciously leave the pieces of information scattered without trying to make sense of them, without organising them into a meaningful image. Be aware, that until you connect with the essence of the place, you are not in a position to organise the fractured pieces of information.*

4. *Next go into a room you feel drawn to and where you will be undisturbed for the next forty five minutes. First focus on setting an intention for your inner journey. It could also be in the form of a question. I suggest that for your first contact with*

the energy of a place you set the intention to get in contact and communicate with its spirit or essence. In a further communication a question may have arisen from a conflict between you and your partner, for example, one wants to demolish the house and the other renovate it. Or, as an architect, you ask the spirit of the place for inspiration with the design. If you are faced with a problem you can ask for advice. The answer to the question should not be 'yes' or 'no' because it is coming from the rational mind. When asking for advice, leave all options open. Sometimes, however, you may receive a very surprising and unexpected intention or question. My shamanic teacher suggested speaking the intention or question out loud, tasting it and mulling over it, until it feels right and 'fits'. Or you may do more than one inner journey.

5. *Now you are ready to go on an inner journey. Sit in a comfortable position and take a few deep breaths. Become aware of your feet firmly on the ground. Relax your whole body from toe to head. Repeat your intention three times and go on your inner journey. You may listen to a steady drum rhythm or just focus on your breath or listen into the silence within. Now imagine your body dissolving into air. There is no separation between you and your surroundings. Next ask a higher being you believe in to be present and support you. Widen the space so that your whole building/place is included. Repeat the following to yourself: "I am asking to get in contact and communicate with the essential quality of my home". Feel the energy. The communication may take the form of images, words or feelings. Accept whatever you experience, including 'nothing'. Stay in this space for ten to*

> *twenty minutes. When you feel the time is up, stay for another minute. Give thanks for what you have received. Then bring your awareness back to the room. Become aware of your feet on the ground. Start to move your feet, then your legs, torso, arms and head. When you are ready, slowly open your eyes.*

The aim of listening to the steady drumming or the rhythm of your heart or your breath is to change the frequency of our brain waves from beta to alpha. In our busy and active daily routine, we are in the beta frequency. When we are anxious we produce too many beta waves. When we close our eyes, our brain starts to produce more alpha waves. Our bodies and minds are relaxed and receptive in this frequency and the information will come through images, colours, feelings, smells or words.

> 6. *Now write down and/or draw what you experienced. Allow your pen to move along the page. You may be surprised by what you bring to paper. Read what you have written out loud. Ask yourself how the experience relates to you and your home. Even when nothing comes, i.e. no information in any form, trust that you are connected to the energy. It may come later when you talk with someone and are surprised at the words that pour out of you. Or the information comes suddenly and unexpectedly at a later point in the form of a sudden insight. If the information you received does not yet give you a full picture, you may need to visit the place again either internally or in physical form.*
>
> 7. *Now that you have come in contact with the spirit of the place, trust that you are connected with the*

> *energy. You will get guidance through intuition, ideas and encounters with other people on how to bring what the energy communicated with you into the material realm. As you are approaching your task with a new sense of wholeness, the support and co-operation of the spirit of the place will manifest in an easy, joyful and efficient process.*

During your inner journey the spirit of the place may have made you aware of blocked energy. You may either have encountered the spirits of deceased former inhabitants or a weak, even broken spirit of the place.

When I came in contact with a spirit in the cottage in Austria, I was afraid. I was entering a new field of reality which I did not know existed. To be afraid is therefore maybe a normal response. Yet, I encourage you not to stop at this point, but to accept the fear, feel it and move on. I will now give you an account of some of the experiences with spirits and how these experiences enriched my life.

We hear more and more about people who were clinically dead and after a short period of time came back and shared their experiences. The American medical doctor Raymond Moody wrote in 1975 in his bestseller "Life after Life"[13] about the transitional stage after the heart has stopped beating.

He states that in a typical near death experience we float upwards, experience ourselves in an out-of-body state, go through a transcendental passage way or tunnel and come into a brilliant warm, loving and accepting light. Deceased friends and relatives are there to support us. A spiritual entity asks: "What have you done with your life?" It is not about worldly success or failure, but how we have learned to love more.

As I have already mentioned above, I had a near death experience when I was suddenly paralysed at the age of 18 months. I recalled this experience later in life as an adult. My understanding is that I wanted to die, because I was overwhelmed with the conflicts of my parents. I was told by a higher spiritual entity that it was not my time yet, that I should go back and that I would get all the support I needed. I felt and feel this support and connection to this day.

I encountered the spirit of the original owner of a place for the first time in the old cottage in the Austrian countryside. I was initially shocked when I felt and saw his presence as I was bringing our baby daughter to bed. I shut down this heightened awareness, partly because of the negative energy of the spirit and partly because I did not know how to deal with the situation.

When my sister and her baby daughter died in a car accident in Italy the following year, I felt her flying above me as I was driving to tell my parents of their daughter's and grandchild's death. While we were waiting for their bodies to be brought back from Italy, my sister appeared to me and told me to get her diaries before our mother could lay hands on them. She was afraid our mother would read her personal accounts and hold on to her even more. Months later I saw her floating in a light blue dress and knew she was free and happy.

Years later, when my mother was sitting at my father's bedside as he was dying, she told me that seconds before he died, he saw me standing at the foot of his bed smiling. He died in a hospital in Vienna, while I was in Ireland, after having visited him the previous week.

During another visit to Vienna, I visited my aunt in her apartment. I asked her if she would support me financially for a course I wanted to attend in America. Suddenly I felt the forbidding presence of my uncle who had died some 10 years previously. I was so shocked that I did not tell my aunt about the encounter. My uncle was strictly against it and my aunt told me that she had given everything to her children. This experience ended all my doubts about the presence of deceased people in our material world.

As my mother's dementia increased she frequently told me about meeting her mother or my sister. Her mother, she explained, would come through a tunnel asking her to go with her, or that my sister would meet us that afternoon.

Few days after her death, my mother would tell me how happy she was. She had met all the deceased relatives and they all had rejoiced in seeing each other again. She contacted me again months later and asked me to find her father, who had died the year before I was born. I went on an inner journey with her. We went deep into the earth through a series of dungeons. The filth and darkness of the place reminded me of prisons in Europe during the Middle Ages. Then we saw my grandfather cowered in the furthest cell, deeply ashamed for something he had done in his life and which had led to his suicide. My mother was very happy to find him. She easily forgave him for his past, which allowed him to get up, take my mother's hand and go with her out into the light. They thanked me and flew off happily into lighter realms.

Months later I heard the phone ringing one night. I was in a dream and at the same time it felt real. I lifted the receiver and knew that it was my mother on the other end. I was afraid as I felt her presence so close and real. I asked her where she was ringing from and she replied, "From heaven". I knew then that I did not need to ask her how she was. We thanked each other for all we had given each other and when there was nothing more to say, I said that we better finish the call as it would be too expensive. She told me that it did not cost anything, but there is a certain time allotted to it. I laughed out loud and with that our conversation ended.

The encounters with my sister's spirit and later with the spirits of others has taught me that it is loving to forgive ourselves for a possible lack of love towards them when they were alive and also to now let them continue on their soul's journey. Contrary to my experience, it is often regarded as loving when we hold on to our dear ones, keep their room intact, go to their grave often, pray for them and grief their loss, especially if they died young or unexpectedly.

I suppose that these personal encounters with close relatives helped me to widen my perception of reality and accept a multidimensional reality as a fact, rather than a myth. These experiences helped me to accept the encounters I will describe below as part of a wider reality. By accepting the presence and grievances of these souls, healing and liberation became possible. The process of getting in contact with energy blocks in a place helps us to become aware of a part of ourselves that is out of alignment. When we acknowledge and accept the information revealed, we have the chance to surrender and to allow the healing take its course.

Based on personal experience, I believe the cause of blocked energy in places and buildings can always be found in wrongs done by past inhabitants. It does not matter if they are still alive or have died a long time ago. Their transgression has blocked the free flow of energy and the spirit of the place. According to Pogacnik, we should tune into the seventh dimension to get in contact with the souls of the people who have lived there before. By acknowledging and accepting both their presence and their deeds, we allow healing to take place.

When we are attracted to a building in which energy is blocked, we can either see it as an opportunity to heal something in us, or reject the invitation for healing, judge it as negative and move on. The world always only offers a mirror. When the relationship with our partner becomes too conflictual, we can always opt out and ask for a divorce. When the space we are living in brings up too many problems, we can decide to move. We always have the free will to reject or embrace the offer. However, most likely the unresolved issues will follow us to the next place, making their presence felt even more strongly and creating bigger conflicts. The following questions are appropriate to ask about the place in which you now live: "What attracted me here in the first place?", "What was my situation at the time?", "How did I leave the previous place?" and "Was the transition peaceful?'

When my task is to design a new building or to alter or extend an existing house, I block out any fantasies or images my mind wants to make up. Instead I go home, let the essence of the energy settle in me and then go on an inner journey at home. My intention is then to ask the energy to support me in designing the building. This is an important point as the energy might advise me to neither design nor build.

The process is always a walk into the unknown, so it is important to trust that you can deal with whatever experience you are faced with. My encounters have shown me that I only come into contact with places whose energy I can deal with.

When I am connected to my soul, which knows neither time nor space, I can get in contact with people who lived in the past or with situations that may happen in the future. Once I am connected to the energy, it does not matter if I am in the specific place, in my office or any other place.

One more thing which I cannot stress enough: Getting in contact with the energy of a place is a mystery. We receive images, we get answers to our questions and somehow everything falls easily into place as we bring ideas into material reality. In the end it is not about the images we receive. It is the mysterious connection with the energy which somehow supports us in our task of designing and building a house or just living in it.

In the following I will share some of my encounters with the energies of places and spaces. I am, however, aware that it is difficult to describe my experiences, without you being able to connect with the energy of the place and feel and experience the process for yourself. I am also aware that you would receive different images and come up with a different design idea. As the energy filters through your unique belief system and personality, the energy expresses itself in different forms and may focus on aspects which are of specific value for you.

I am including these personal experiences as they might give you a sense of how the process of connecting to the energy of a place works and that each place has its unique energy.

6. BLOCKED ENERGIES AND THEIR HEALING

When the inner and the outer merge miracles occur.

Hildegard von Bingen

In this section I will give an account of working in places where the energy was blocked. As I said before, the outer always mirrors the inner. Therefore there is always a correlation between the energy of the place and the energy of the people who were originally attracted to the place. When the reason for the blocked energy is brought to the clients' awareness, it is still their free will whether they want to let go of the sickness for which the house or place serves as a mirror.

Vienna, Austria

Angry,
    Resentful,
        Intent to take revenge.

It was in 1946, one year after the war, when my mother found an apartment to rent. Living space was a rarity after all the bombings. My parents had married and moved into an apartment in a Jewish quarter of the city. A Jewish family had lived there before the war and now the apartment was empty. Even though we knew this, we never inquired as to what had happened to this family.

I only did this 60 years later, when my mother moved out of the apartment. In a few quiet moments I said farewell to the apartment and expressed my gratitude for the years I had lived in it as a child.

Suddenly I became aware of an energetic presence. It was the spirit of the couple who had originally lived in the apartment. Their energy had been present all those years. They were very angry, resentful and intent to take revenge for the pain and injustice done to them during the Nazi regime. I apologised to them and expressed my sympathy. They started to soften and were able to let go of their grievances, leave the apartment and move into lighter dimensions.

My childhood was full of conflicts. My maternal grandmother was half Jewish and her husband a Nazi. This unsolved conflict of my grandparents, representing both victim and victimiser, certainly had an influence on why my mother had found this apartment. Looking back, I can see that I too always carried this conflict within me. My best friend as a child was Jewish and I felt guilty for half my life for something that had happened before I was born. It seems that the unresolved conflicts of one generation are carried over to the next. As long as they remain hidden in the unconscious, they live on and call for healing in the generations to follow.

Cottage and shed, County Mayo, Ireland

Hunchback of Cogaula,
  Brocken by the English landlord.

The client is originally from England and is managing an Irish company in County Mayo. He is considering buying land with an old house and the remains of stables. My intention for the inner journey is to communicate with the spirit of the land.

When I did the inner journey, I had already made a sketch design and found out that there was broken limestone two foot beneath the surface.

I meet the spirit who introduces himself as "The Hunchback of Cogaula". He tells me that his spirit was broken by the English landlord like the stone two feet below the surface of the land. I listen carefully and accept what he is telling me. Suddenly, he stands proud and straight, open to the sun like the centre part of my house design with arms wide outstretched, holding the past and honouring it.

"How come you suddenly stand so straight?" I ask.

He replies that I have come and healed him by communicating with him and also through my design, which reflects his pride and strength. He is very happy with the design (which connects the two existing parts with a circular living room which opens with a glass front to the south).

"What is your name now?" "I am the Proud and Erect Spirit of Cogaula", re-erected thanks to you, listening to my story and thereby releasing my pain. I am so very grateful to you."

He finishes by saying that my client will be healed as well. "He is as broken as I was."

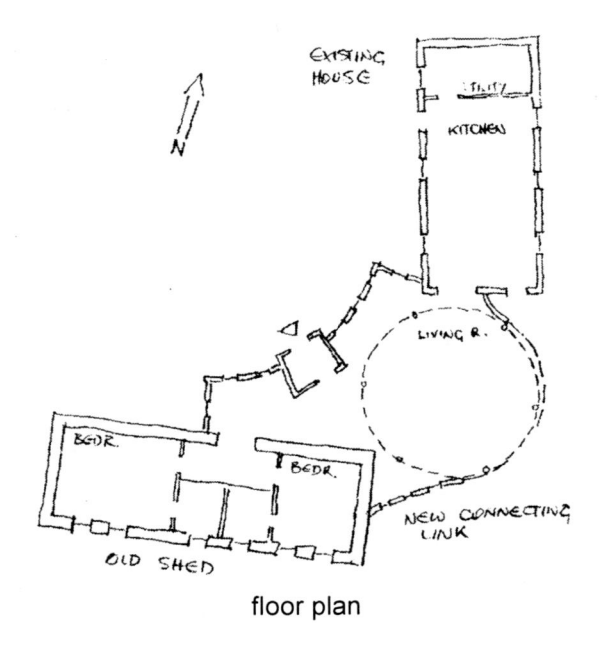

floor plan

A few weeks later the process was ended. The client couldn't afford to continue the project as the company he managed had to shut down due to the bubble burst in property. His company was in the building trade.

How does this relate to the information I had received? The client's brokenness became apparent on more than one level, including his private life and the breakup of his relationship. Did healing happen for him as well? I don't know. While the communication with the energy of the place indicates a clear connection with the client, who was drawn to the place, our relationship did not continue. Was there a connection between the client being an Englishman and the spirit broken by an English landlord?

How communications on an astral level (higher invisible energy level) play out in our physical life is beyond my control. It lies within the free will of the person, if they want to accept the healing and subsequent changes in their life or not. It may also have had consequences and brought changes to the owner of the land which I am not aware of.

By connecting energetically to a place, we can restore the power of the essential energy of the place. But this is only the first step. We then have to bring the matrix/essence/spirit down into physical reality. We can compare this process to baking a cake: we can choose the best recipe, but we still need to get the ingredients and bake the cake in order to transform the instructions and ingredients into a real cake. We can also choose not to bake the cake. Reality is a field of potentiality. What we choose to manifest in the physical form is our free choice.

Existing house, Co. Mayo, Ireland

See me,
    Talk to me,
        Honour my beauty.

The house stands on a small piece of land with a deep fall to a lake. The rear of the house offers a magnificent view over the lake and beyond. The house itself is damp and feels neglected. The clients want to buy the house and wonder if they should renovate and extend it or tear it down. There is also the question whether to buy more land from a neighbour as the site is rather small.

My following inner journey gives answers to their questions:

I become aware of the presence of the spirit of the place underneath the house. It appears black and slightly threatening. He says he is angry. The people who originally lived there were very negative and the new ones very seldom live there. No one appreciates him for his beauty... He is suddenly lighter, not black anymore and has almost moved up to ground level while I have been listening to and talking with him.

He says that under no circumstances should I suggest to build a new house. He would go underground and undermine all efforts. The image of connecting the house and shed with a conservatory appears. I am informed that the origin of the dampness is in the roof and gutter. I am advised to measure the house and recommend conserving it. More land wouldn't help. At the end the spirit tells me his name is Alex.

You may wonder about the name and may judge it as childish or downright stupid. So, why would I still mention it? Firstly, because this was the communication I received. It does not make sense to argue and doubt the communication. I know the rational critical mind thrives on arguing and doubting. Secondly, communicating with the energy of a place creates intimacy and connection. It is, therefore, natural to know its name and use it.

To return now to the inner journey. The communication with the energy of the house and place is on two levels: an emotional and a practical level. Whatever took place while the original owners lived there, they did not appreciate the beauty of the place. This negative energy may have led to the next owner avoiding the place. But listening to the grievances and accepting them, leads to a dissolution of the negative energies and a willingness of the energy to cooperate by giving advice. On a very practical level building a new house with heavy machinery on an extremely steep site could have resulted in the weakening of the bedrock and caused consequent problems during the building process.

An experienced engineer may have come to the same conclusion. However, I am now energetically connected to the place having received the information by communicating with the spirit. A living relationship is established and this allows for cooperation to develop which serves all parties involved. This specific cooperation started with practical and detailed advice on the next steps to take.

The clients were an Irish couple living in England. I only ever communicated with the wife, whose brother lived close by. Her husband favoured the idea of demolishing the old house and building a new one. I never had a chance to meet both of them together. The process didn't go any further as they decided not to buy and remain living in England. Why? They never told me and I did not want to pry.

During the process the financial crisis and the consequent collapse of the building industry in Ireland may have changed their original outlook. There are many more possible explanations and assumptions that could be made. Once we acknowledge that reality is multidimensional we become aware of the many reasons and must concede that we cannot possibly know all of them nor do not need to know them. But the rational mind gets very irritated when it cannot wrap it all up in a neat package (mine at least does).

House in County Mayo, Ireland

Outer clutter mirrors inner chaos.
   Persistent inner work
     Rekindles the fire.
         A little willingness is essential.

I enter an old cottage with an existing extension. It is situated in the country side with a wide peaceful view to the north. My first impression of the house is that it is cluttered. It has altogether 3 bathrooms and 3 bedrooms. The part of the old stone cottage has 2 bedrooms and 2 bathrooms and a central living room. The central chimney flue in the living room has collapsed and the fire place is therefore out of use. There is also an extension to the South, with a kitchen and another bathroom and corridor. The energy is one of confusion. The client smokes frequently and is nervous and confused.

She has already asked an architect for a design for a new extension instead of the existing one, but is not happy with the proposal, including the idea of bringing light into the living room with a roof light. Confused as what to do next, she asks me for my opinion.

I sit down on my own in the living room and close my eyes with the intention of getting in contact with the spirit of the house.

After some inner journeying, I land in the house and fall down into the earth. I land in a cave with seven dwarfs who are busy working. I feel a deep sense of peace and security.

Conclusion: The living room in the old part is the womb and anchor of the house. A roof light would therefore create a conflict with the energy of the room. The seven dwarfs make aware of the inner work the client needs to do in order to anchor herself. They also point out that the building supports the client in this inner work and that the reward will be peace and security.

I consequently suggest that she connects for seven days with the energy by visualising the cave and to allow the seven dwarfs to do their work. By establishing this inner womb and core, she will feel safe and carry that into the south facing extension, where she feels lonely at the moment. At the same time I suggest that the clutter be cleared and the house cleaned. I propose that we meet again in two weeks and talk about the experience she has had in the meantime. I see myself as the bridge between the spirit of the house and the client and suggest that I support her in embodying the energy of the house.

She rang me the next day to tell me that she didn't want to continue the work with me. She did not tell me the reason and I did not ask her. I decided just to accept her "no".

I see her house as a gift from heaven to her, as it offers her all that she needs to overcome her feelings of loneliness and confusion. She has reminded me of how often I would have rejected something life has offered me, because I have thought it is too much work, costs too much or because I had some other 'clever' idea and have thereby missed seeing the gift.

7. ENERGIES ON A PERSONALITY LEVEL

In the encounters described above we have witnessed the energy blocks in places and also how they can be liberated. When this happens, the personality or special quality of the place comes to life again. This mirrors our own potential for transformation. When we are able to let go of our grievances, anger and sadness, we can then share our talents and special gifts and the uniqueness of our personality.

Landscapes and their places can reflect back to us feelings which are elevating or depressing, dark or light, fertile or barren, challenging or relaxing. And just as landscapes have their unique character, so too have individual places. They can be motherly and nourishing, or stern and challenging. They can be virgin and innocent, or dark and mysterious. They mirror the different personality traits within us.

Once the energy blocks of a place are removed and the energy can flow freely again, the strength and unique character of the place can radiate and express itself.

The place can become our teacher or a safe nest after it has been released of blocked energy. When both a dark and a light image are present in a place, we can ask ourselves if we are open and willing to acknowledge the darkness inside us as well as nourish the joyful.

In the following section I will give a few examples of the unique 'personality' traits of places with which I have connected.

Biberbach, Austria

The house as a teacher:
  Align to the rhythm of the seasons,
    Go back to basics
      And know your place in the big picture.

When I lived in Vienna where I met my wife Bettina, we felt we could no longer live in a city. We were drawn to look for a house in the countryside and bought a small cottage on one and a half acres of land. We fell in love with the little house, in which I had to bow low to pass through each doorway. And we were charmed by the meadow around that bloomed in early summer with a wide variety of wildflowers.

The first night we spent in the house Bettina dreamed that its spirit was our teacher. It told her that she should stay in the house, otherwise she would remain an observer all her life. After we had a closer look at the house the following day, we considered pulling out of buying the house. Everywhere we looked, we saw 'problems': the water from the kitchen tap came from a drain, the bath was not connected to a water supply, the stove was smoking and we wondered how the old furniture was ever brought into the room.

But we stayed on and over the next four years the house and its surroundings helped us reconnect with ourselves, our roots, the earth and the rhythm of the seasons. We had a garden and sowed our first seeds, planted trees, kept sheep and chickens and felt the fear of the lamb when we brought it to the neighbour to be slaughtered.

When my sister unexpectedly died in a car accident, owls sat in trees next to the house grieving with us. It made me aware that I was not isolated from my environment and that nature was connected with me much more than I ever thought possible.

After we had cleared and cleaned the house, and then written a book about our experience of moving from a city to the countryside, we were ready to move on.

What did we learn from this house? It taught us simplicity, what our basic needs were, and if I didn't want to bang my head against the low door frame, I had to learn humility. And it wasn't just the door frame I banged my head against, when life didn't go my way!

When we visited the house a few years later, the next owner had upgraded the house to today's living standards and at the same time honoured its spirit and connection to the earth. The owner from whom we had bought it had saved the old stone cottage from collapse and decay. We cleaned and cleared it and today, almost hidden between sunflowers, bushes and trees, it is witness to a magic connection to the earth. It is an oasis within a 'desert' of modern farmers and industrialized farming, with cattle kept inside all year round and manicured meadows without any "weeds", i.e. wild flowers.

Land in County Mayo, Ireland

White, light,
    Delicate, feminine spirit
        Dancing in the shape of an eight.

The client asks me to plan a house on a piece of land owned by a relative at the time. The intention of my inner journey was to communicate with the spirit of the place.

I jump into our lake, come to a sea shore, swim in the sea, fly up towards the heavens, become one with the sun, fall down to earth and land on the place in question.

Dark, stone, watery;
something emerges.
A white, light,
delicate, feminine spirit
dancing in the shape of an eight.
I want to ask her name.
She asks me to dance with her.
I become her.
I dance the figure eight.
It is soothing.
"Bring 'delicate' into the design of the place.
Plant birch trees."
I am asked to continue dancing with her while designing the house.
(I make sketches and bring to paper the idea of the design)
She tells me her name is Acara.
I carry her with me,
embody her, as I design.

ENERGIES ON A PERSONALITY LEVEL

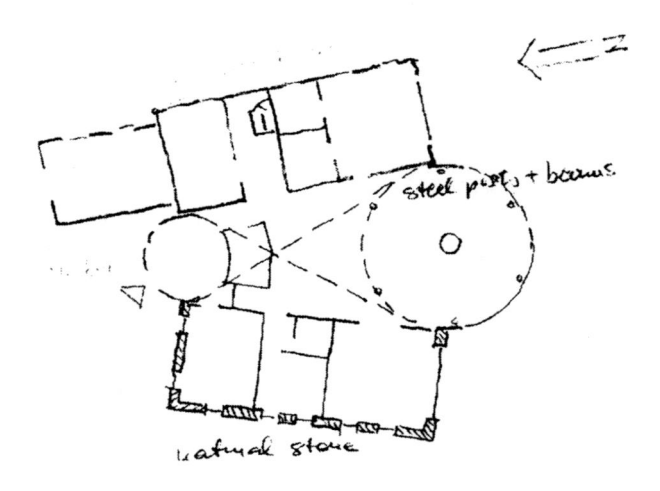

floor plan

The connection with the energy continued throughout the planning process. It was actually one of the best examples how the energy of a place contains and cooperates with the design of a building (the centre of the house is in the form of the figure eight with thin steel posts in the circular living room) and the surrounding environment (advice to plant birch trees).

The name of the place is 'Happy Meadow', which captures the spirit of the place and shows that people in previous times were aware of the energy of places and their quality.

I did not communicate this information directly with my client. But I expressed the spirit of the place in the design and he was very happy with it. The relationship with the client was very amiable and the designing process went very smooth for most of the process. It was towards the end of the planning process that the spirit of the design got lost and only the form remained.

The timber and steel structure of the central figure eight was replaced with a concrete ceiling and the planned green roof with a plastic membrane. My input had ended with the planning permission and the project became one of my greatest professional disappointments. It subsequently became a great lesson in detachment and letting go of the sense of ownership I claimed through my design and energy work. It taught me that I can only do my part and must let go of expectations of how others might decide and behave.

Land in County Mayo

Caring,
    Embracing,
        Nourishing
Mother.

I was asked as an architect to design a modern family home on a 13 acre site. Right from the beginning there was trust and connection between the client and me. I initially designed a house and stables for horses, which the clients loved, but the planners rejected.

Despite this rejection, the clients still wanted me to design their family home. This time I got in contact with the spirit of the place, which appeared to me in the image of a caring loving mother. After this first communication, I felt connected to the place and felt an invisible support from and cooperation with the energy for my work.

From that point onwards, everything went smoothly. I was willing to cooperate with the planners and their critique actually improved the quality of the design. For example, the part of the house which faces the road is based on a traditional cottage.

elevation

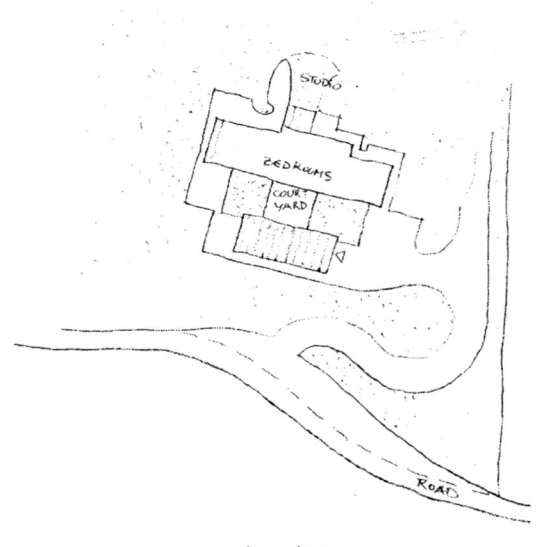

site plan

Even though the house is big with a floor area of 350 m2, it looks small from the road. It is designed around an inner court yard, built in steps into the hill and the studio is situated right into the earth with a grass roof blending into the existing landscape. During the building process every decision was made in communication with the client, the different contractors and the tradesmen. While most building processes are stressful, this has been enjoyable and exiting from beginning to end.

The clients moved into the house at a time when there was still no flooring, no heating or interior doors. They were happy, despite these short comings. Since then they have made it their home at their own pace and according to their own taste. Without ever talking to them about the energy of the place, they connected to the friendly supportive motherly energy of the place through their intense involvement during the design and building stages. The woman of the house embodies this loving caring energy.

House and land in County Mayo, Ireland

Dark and light,
  nature and cosmic spirits
    unite the couple's opposing ideas.

A couple with two girls own the house and land. The house is on a lane which cuts through the middle of the declining strip of land. On the top of this strip of land one can see Croagh Patrick, Ireland's holy mountain. At the bottom of the hill the site ends at a small lake. There is a grove of trees beside the house. At the time of consultation the couple had two opposing ideas. He wanted to sell and move to another place. She wanted to stay and use the land for gardening and also as a Retreat Centre. This was only one example of the sometimes conflicting relationship of the couple. They both asked me to sense the energy and quality of the place to help them find an answer.

ENERGIES ON A PERSONALITY LEVEL

I consequently went on a Shamanic Journey with the intention of getting in contact with the spirit of their place, including the lake. It was a unique experience that the essence of the place spoke directly to the owners, using me as the messenger. The spirit gave clear instructions about what had to be done.

*The Spirit of the place shows itself in form of a
black jellyfish with many arms reaching out in
all directions. The spirit of the lake appears as a
delicate, dancing female figure, dressed in white.
Create a focus point on top of the hill (with
view to the mountain, Crough Patrick), maybe
create a gazebo, as a meditation space.
Create pathways from the conservatory
to both the gazebo and the lake.
Create some clearing around the lake.
Include the girls. Encourage them to
communicate with the fairies in the forest.
Create a kind of altar in the conservatory that connects
to all three places (top of the hill, lake and fairy place)
to hold these three energy fields in awareness.
Clean sheds and mobile home.
Possibly move the mobile home. Mobile home
could serve as guest accommodation.
Create an open space/meeting place
between road and lake.
Axis along sheds and road connects to outer world.
Create orchard and area for sheep. Clean and clear
space of former polytunnel and possibly restore.
Once you have established the above mentioned
energy points, follow your inspiration.
The darkness of the spirit of the land is not negative. It
represents a deep grounding, balanced by the light spirit of
the lake, the joyful spirit of the fairies and the spot on top of
the hill, which connects to the spiritual light of Croagh Patrick.*

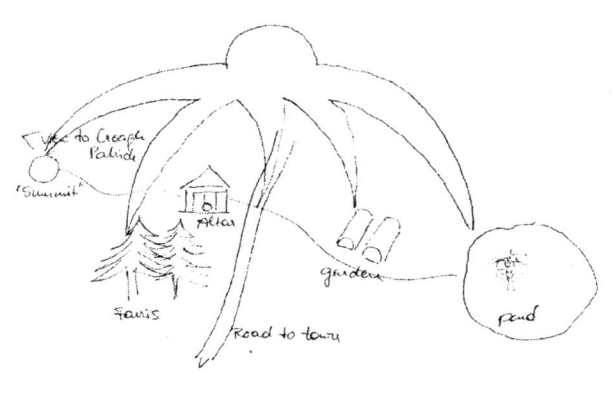

Spirit of place

The land represents and mirrors the family dynamic. The dark and light forces of the lake and land mirror the dynamic of the couple. Their two girls embody the fairies, which live in a grove of trees near the house. With the help of the spiritual light (the high frequency of energy) of Croagh Patrick, this place could be ideal to heal the relationships within the family.

They bought house and land at the height of the property boom and have not been able to sell it. What is it that keeps them living there? Is it the depressed property market, the magnetic attraction of the place's energy or the call for healing of their souls?

Having recently got in contact with the woman again, I learned how the place has changed the family and they in turn have changed the place. In the intervening five years they have restored the organic garden, planted wildflowers around the conservatory and a ring of trees on top of the hill, on the spot which connects their land energetically to the holy mountain of Crough Patrick. In the meantime their daughter and nephew have both seen the image of the female figure, dressed in white, dancing on the lake and their older daughter often sees the nature spirits in the little grove. Both parents originally came from England and Northern Ireland and have now settled in the place and continue to make it their home. They have become aware of their own inner darkness, have befriended it and now enjoy a better relationship with each other.

The couple told me that the place was a soup kitchen in famine times, where hungry people often lost their way when travelling in search of the nearby sea. To this day the area is a kind of Bermuda triangle, where people still lose their way and are helped by friendly locals out of the maize of roads (this has also happened to me). The place has supported them in grounding themselves and finding a way out of the maize of their life.

It is a challenging but rich place, where all aspects are present: the dark side calling for healing and grounding, but also the support of both nature spirits and light energy for acceptance and transformation of the dark energy.

House in Hamburg, Germany

An egg,
    A closed blossom,
        A nest.
           Whole in itself.

The owners of the house are an elderly couple, whose children have long left home. The house feels very cosy and homely. While she does not want any changes, he is restless and wants an extension built onto the house.

In an inner journey I see the energy of the house in the image of an egg, a closed blossom, a nest. It is whole in itself. *The client's idea of extending it to the rear would be like a cancerous growth as the energy of the egg/nest is whole and does not need any outer extensions.*

He can accept my findings. The conflict and uncertainty are resolved.

Had I approached the task in the normal architectural contract, I would have made a sketch design and even gone further. I would not only have wasted time and effort, but the resulting conflict may have manifested in me having to fight for my fee and the client not wanting to pay. There could have been an endless list of conflicts during the whole process. It could also have shown in conflicts between the couple as the opinion of his wife would have been ignored. Delays and mistakes during the building process would have been another common outcome. By getting in contact with the essential quality of a place, we can avoid all of these conflicts.

House in Gästrikland, Sweden

Honour those who have gone before you.
Transform their heavy load into a simple smile.

Visiting friends in Sweden, I came in contact with a house that was built some 150 years ago. Only two rooms were ever made habitable, the remaining 80% of the house was never finished. It was a very simple and solid house: no decoration, only massive wood beams and boards, and stone and iron. The owners, our friends, each had a very different relationship with the house.

He felt connected to the house and was in a process of renovating, upgrading and finishing it. His goal was to stay in tune with the soul of the house by respecting its simplicity and bareness and, instead of adding round shapes or building on a conservatory, just leave its square and simple structure intact. The only change he wanted to make was to make the house 'proud' by curving the roof 'to make it smile'. His partner, however, was unhappy and lonely there and wanted to either move or extend it into a yoga retreat centre, where people would come and stay there for days or a week.

They asked me to get in touch with the soul of the house to find common ground in their opposing perceptions.

I meditate, see myself in the house and sink into the rock beneath the house, deeper and deeper into darkness. The darkness is alive with many entities who are all busy working. I become aware of people on the ground floor. They are wearing working clothes the colour of the stone. They have worked with stone all their life, which has been heavy work.

Then my legs are pulled deeper and deeper into the dark rock, stretching my lower body immensely, while my torso and head stay above the ground in the light. Snow White and the seven dwarfs pop up. I am told to investigate the meaning of Snow White with our friends; especially with the woman. Afterwards I feel refreshed and deeply grounded.

Later I present my inner journey to my friends in the form of a guided meditation in which they get in touch with the energy as I have felt it. We talk about the fairy tale and how the busy entities in the rock support her in grounding herself. She can feel the support from the earth below without being sucked into the darkness. The people on the ground floor represent the original builders and owners of the house. Most likely they were too busy working for survival and had neither the time nor the means to finish the house. They also explain the roughness, sturdiness and simplicity of the house. By finishing the house, our friends honour and respect the hardship of these people at a time, where many people from all over Europe had to emigrate in order to survive.

Months later our friends contacted me. The woman told me that she felt settled and happy in the house for the first time, while he was finishing the house, making it proud with a smiling roof. They built the yoga centre upstairs together, which was the first time she got involved in the building process. Her yoga centre is thriving as she is having more groups than ever before.

A site in Carinthia, Austria

No,
No,
No. Get off!

Friends of ours had bought a site overlooking a lake in Austria. A local architect had made a design, but the couple was not happy with it. He had bought the land, but she wondered if she would ever want to move there. They were both living in Dublin at the time and were about to move back to Germany, or settle on this site in Austria. They asked me for my advice. As I needed to see and feel the place in person, we travelled there together.

We arrived in the evening and as it was late autumn, it was already dark. Nonetheless, I followed my impulse and we went to the site immediately after arrival.

The place is extremely steep and does not appear to be a building site at all. I connect with the earth by asking the

ENERGIES ON A PERSONALITY LEVEL

question: "How do you feel about my friends' wish to build and live here?" The immediate answer is: "Very unhappy. We will prick you with our thorns. We are already hurt by the neighbour, who built on the left side". It is very difficult to climb on to the site. Acacias have grown wild and I cannot avoid being pricked by their thorns. I get the feeling that the neighbouring steep slope will further erode.

When we came back in clear daylight the following day, I saw the neighbouring site with a big two storey house and a very high concrete wall behind to protect the slope from sliding. I learned that the sub-soil is gravel all the way down. No wonder the house above, even though situated further up, had cracks in the walls because of the movement of the loose gravel underground.

Communicating with the energy, walking the land and being aware of the thorns which clearly said: "get off!" and then listening to the neighbours' experiences and the subsequent conflicts gave us rich information on multiple levels. The answer to the question, whether they should build and live there, was a very, very clear "no". It obviously should have never been designated as a building site by the town council in the first place.

Walking the site at night was an interesting experience. The contact with the energy was simple and clear, without any need to meditate or prepare a space for an inner journey. At night the physical reality loses its dominance and the veil to other dimensions gets very thin. The soul is wide open to receive and inform us.

Our friends were lucky to find a buyer five years later when they had already settled in Germany. There was no way to solve this problem as it was not suited as a building site. The new buyer will have to deal with the resulting conflict.

8. ENERGIES OF HIGHER FREQUENCY

Based on my personal experiences I believe that the earth and all on it, within it and above it are connected and interdependent. The earth is therefore not an isolated globe, but connected within our solar system and our galaxy and beyond with the whole universe.

We have created power networks around the globe which enable us to get electricity or gas directly into our homes, offices and public spaces. Communication networks enable us to get in contact with the rest of our world via phone or internet. More recently, satellites from space allow us to communicate with each other from almost any place on the earth. These satellites and secret agencies receive detailed information about their perceived enemies.

These man-made networks are imitations of information and power networks that have existed for thousands if not millions of years. Shamans, High Priests and Initiates knew about them, used them and as caretakers protected them from negative and destructive energies. These sacred sites and power points are connected to each other around the globe through invisible power lines. They receive universal energy and channel this energy into the earth.

These power lines are called lay lines or dragon lines, and vortices, situated at their intersections, funnel universal energy into the earth and connect to Gaia, the spirit of the earth, the light at the centre of the earth. Vortices are whirlpools or funnels which draw particles of energy together in a spinning motion and concentrate them. An Indian swastika, seen in fourth dimension (in time and motion), moves in clockwise direction. It symbolizes constructive life energy. A Nazi swastika was black and moved in anti-clockwise direction as a destructive symbol. A tornado moves also anti-clockwise and causes destruction in its path.

These power points then inform and empower the development of places, landscapes, towns, cities and regions by providing matrices or blueprints.

Indigenous peoples and cultures across the globe were familiar with these power lines. Ancient sites, such as Newgrange in Ireland, Stonehenge in England, Hallstadt in Austria are examples of intersections along these power lines. Later on, early Christian churches and monasteries in Europe were built on ancient places of worship, for example, Chartres in France, Cologne cathedral in Germany, Hagia Sophia in Istanbul or St. Peters in Rome. All these famous buildings were built on the ruins of pre-Christian sacred places. Almost all monasteries and churches were built on these ancient power places. With the decline of religious power and the rise of a secular society, the new powers of Nation states used these power lines for their own ends and with the help of Geomancy, connected into this power grid.

One example, as I experienced, is the street planning along the Mall in Washington DC, USA. The Washington Monument receives universal energy from the universe, which is then channelled to Capitol Hill, the White House, the Pentagon and, via the Reflecting Pool, to the Lincoln Memorial. Most, if not all, European cities are connected through lay lines to the flow of universal energy. The intelligence within the energy informs them with a matrix (blueprint) and allows them to grow and change.

Nature has another powerful energy network. In Ireland these communication points are in fairy ring forts. These are places where nature spirits live and inform and empower the natural world of plants and animals. These 'Nature Power Places' are marked with shrines of the Virgin Mary across continental Catholic Europe, where the spirit of the earth is revered through Mary.

The information above provides some background and context to understand the examples I give below. I did not go into great detail about the energy of these sites, as it is not the focus of this book.

The next two examples contain all three elements: the clearing of energies, the personality of the place and its higher purpose. I chose to include these two examples here to highlight that blocked energy first has to be brought back into flow, so that the personality of a place can be freely expressed. Only then can the higher purpose start to be fulfilled. As it is with places, so too with us humans. We also have to look at our shadows and release them so that our personality can shine at its best. Only then are we ready to fulfil our life's purpose and our soul's deepest longing.

Lough Rusheen, Castlebar, County Mayo, Ireland

The place and the caretakers become one.
What is cleared on the outside,
Mirrors a clearing within
As one supports the other
And gets supported in return.

This place is an exception to the other examples given insofar, as Bettina and I have lived here for almost 30 years. In these years the place supported us and we supported the place. We transformed the place and the place supported us in our transformation. For 20 years we brought energy blocks back into flow both within ourselves and in the land. The constantly changing sky and lake, the steady, almost indiscernible growth of the bog, the brown heather protecting the earth on top of a hill, but itself exposed to the wild storms. These constant opposites express the personality of the place and mirror Bettina's and my personality as a couple. Only when the blocked energy within us and in the place was cleared, did I discover a higher frequency of energy in the centre of the place. It may have been always there and attracted me to the place in the first place. But I was only now ready to open myself and became aware of it.

One weekend a group of eleven people gathered on our land to recite and write poetry. At one stage we went out onto the land and to its centre, where I had marked an intersection of lay lines[14] with a small acrylic dome. We visualized light energy forming a whirlpool or vortex bringing the light down into the bog and beyond and creating a light cathedral. We set an intention for an answer to a question we had concerning our lives at that moment.

We let our intentions go and let ourselves be inspired by the light energy, the open bog, the lake, the mountains and the nature spirits. As an answer to my question: "What does this new unknown 'playing field' in my life look like?' the following came:

*The new playing field
is vast and boundless
with no road or path.*

*And yet a gentle pull
will firmly guide you
showing you the way.
Be easy, playful, happy
so not to miss direction.
Ideas born from thin air
you are transforming
into words, images and dense matter.
Dense energies are brought to light
to rise and flow once more.
There is only the moment
and what you need to know
will be known to you.*

Then I sat down in the forest we had planted in the beginning and leaned against a tree which swayed in the wind, right down to its roots. I moved with it back and forth while emptying my thoughts.

*The wind blows through my body
and leaves my mind empty.
Light and shadows dance
on the soft needle floor,
where I rest for a while.
I need to know nothing.
The energy flows through my legs
Up from the ground.
My shoulders relax.
Nothing to do, nowhere to go.
Tree tops are dancing, trunks moving with the wind
around a blue sky
bending, aching, singing
without a no or but or why, nor ever why me or poor me,
Only yes, yes, yes.*

I could not have said or done any of the above 30 years ago when we moved to these twenty acres of bog land, with deep holes made by cattle trampling through the soft ground, searching for grass between the heather and the moss. There wasn't a single tree on the site, no road or pathway, electricity or water supply. I perceived the land as a damp desert that gave me the freedom to follow my dream of transforming it into a natural park and with no obligation to animals to keep the grass short.

As I said before, digging the land to build some drains, a road and a foundation, I not only dug up the earth but also unleashed my fears of survival and hunger, my feelings of abandonment as a stranger in a strange land, my feelings of sadness, loss and resentment about injustices done to me in the past. Beginning a new, pioneering adventure also brought up the old, cultural conditioning. Our dreams of starting a new life with a lot of energy and enthusiasm, gave way to a huge culture shock after two years.

Once we moved from the caravan into the house, we started to relax. Leaning back in the rudiments of our new home, we dared to confess to ourselves that everything in this new country was strange and different. We continued to build the rest of our home and got connected to power and water supply and a phone line. Only then did we feel ready to acknowledge our culture shock and do something about it. Parallel to the furnishing of the interior of the house we started an inner journey of inquiring into the architecture of our mind.

During the time of building the shell of the house with timber and glass all my existential fears manifested as mistakes which later needed to be repaired. As the house has an unusual design with round shapes and a 'green' roof and a geodesic dome, the design and construction demanded great patience and attention to detail. However, in my panic and impatience to get things done before the next storm or rain or the approaching winter, I often did not connect to the stillness within, which contained all the answers.

Once we lived in the house, I started to calm down and after building two German stoves using firebricks and lime mortar, I gained confidence in venturing into the unknown. I had a basic knowledge of the principles of such stoves and worked without any plans or drawings. I only knew where the flue should connect into the chimney and allowed the shape of the stove to unfold day by day as I put three or four bricks into place. Thirty years later this hearth (heart) is still working and heating the living room. A second stove heats a room we use for group gatherings and other such activities.

So each part of the house still holds the energy and consciousness of the time it was built. Building my own house made me aware of the importance of consciousness during the building process and of the consequences for future generations of inhabitants. In later years my top priority as an architect was to create a flowing, trusting relationship between architect, client and contractors. Consequently conflicts and problems were addressed which resulted in a harmonious and fulfilling process for all involved.

I learned how my mind worked and subsequently cleared my unhappiness producing beliefs. With a mixture of curiosity, excitement and perseverance, I repaired and renewed the architecture of my mind.

We continued our inner work with the help of the "Option Dialogue Process" and its Socratic questioning process (which I explained in chapter 3). We became aware of burdens on the land as I mentioned before. When we first came to the land there was a heap of dried turf near the road, which neighbours eventually removed. After that they never greeted us. Years later I saw the film 'The Field', where an American wants to buy a field from a woman who has leased it to a local farmer on a long-term basis. This farmer has fertilised it year after year by carrying seaweed from the shore to the field. The conflict ends in murder and tragedy.

After seeing the film I approached one of our neighbours and asked him why he and his brothers never greet us. I learned from him that four neighbours had the right to cut turf on our land and that they felt betrayed by the auctioneer and his solicitor, who had sold us the land. It took years of listening, perseverance and good will to remove the burdens. When all issues were finally settled, the neighbour, who had refused to enter our house, sat down with us and relaxed with a cup of tea in the conservatory. We became friends in the process of clearing old issues and listening to the stories of injustice and betrayal.

A few years later, we asked an energy healer to check our place. He found many souls gathered in our living room in front of the open fire place, still resenting the pain and hardships from the famine years in the middle of the 19th century. In one corner of the land, where an old cottage had once stood, he found a very angry soul, who still wanted revenge for the hardship and injustice done to him. All the years since arriving here, we danced the dance of lack of forgiveness, hardship and anger with these spirits. After he had cleared the energy, I asked him if he would take me on as his student. While he agreed, but my apprenticeship was not at all what I had expected.

I became a student, then a practitioner and eventually a counsellor of shamanism[15], e.g. I connected with invisible inner or other worlds. Subsequently, I became aware of an intersection of lay lines in the centre of the place. While meditating on this intersection, I intuited to mark it with a dome. I looked on the internet for domes of about six meters in diameter, big enough for groups of people to gather underneath. While I was planning to build a dome, I began to wonder how all the material could be brought to a one meter deep bog, with no road leading to the spot. It all seemed too complicated and also too destructive to the unique and pristine character of the land. I decided against removing all the bog and building a road to the energy point.

Each time, however that I communicated with the energy at the centre of the land, the answer came to mark the spot with a dome. One day I checked again on the internet and saw a side advertisement for a cheap, light, transparent and elegant polyester dome, two feet in diameter. I couldn't believe my eyes! I got stones from a quarry and on a sunny summer day dug down to the clay with a group of eight people, laid a dry stone wall in a circle, which soon filled up with water and then closed the 'well' with the dome. Now the two bands of energy could form a vortex[16] and thereby channel the energy from the lay lines down into the earth. Two years later I saw the image of a cathedral of light beneath the dome.

During all these years the development of the land was a mirror of my own inner transformation. When we came to the land it was peaceful, with a wide view all around. It was situated on the margin between wilderness and agricultural land. There are now around 3,000 thirty-year-old trees, bushes, flowers, areas of green grass with daisies, dandelions and clover, frogs and ducks, foxes, hares, pheasants and herons, doves and cuckoo to name but a few. We facilitate regular writing, drumming and singing groups here in a specially built room in the house and provide space for other gatherings of people with a different focus. People from the area and the nearby town now come to use the area along the lake for walking or fishing.

In February frogs come jumping from all directions to mate and lay their eggs in the pond in front of the house. When the tadpoles start swimming, the wild ducks come from the lake and feed on them. During the winter, geese arrive each time before it gets cold. Before they leave at the end of winter they gather on the lake, fly in formation once around the lake, then leave to spend the summer to northern countries. The doves come back from the south in late spring. The cuckoo sings to mark the beginning of summer. Seagulls lay their eggs on stumps of oak in the lake. Flowers and bushes are in bloom at certain times during the longer days of the year. When the first whiff of autumn is in the air, it is time to bring in the firewood for the winter and stack new logs to dry.

We have transformed the place and the place supports us in our transformation. We see ourselves as care takers and the place takes care of us and gives us a home.

I connect daily to the energy of the centre of the place and go there from time to time to connect and receive messages or answers to questions. I believe it is important not only to create connection but also to nurture it regularly with our thoughts and intentions. What we focus on gets bigger. And energy follows thought. It is with intention and focus that we create what we want to manifest.

County Galway, Ireland

All in all I had three contacts with the energy of this place. The first contact with the energy of the house removed the energy block. The second inner journey showed the personality of the place and helped me with the design process. The third communication revealed the quality and purpose of the place now that the people are living in the house. Whether the owners choose to cooperate with the place and avail of the support, is their decision.

But let us start with the first contact where I removed the energy block.

Siblings cast out by relatives
  Ashamed of them being different.

> *Welcome their anger,*
>   *Suppressed for so long.*

The house is situated in a very remote area in County Galway right at the sea overlooking a bay. It is an old stone cottage. The clients tell me about the history of the house. The house is very damp with green mould on the walls; in the bathroom and kitchen also on the ceiling. The previous owners were apparently aware of the problem and tried to solve it by rendering the inside walls with cement mortar, which were originally bare stone walls. They filled the holes in the outside stone walls with cement mortar, too. All of this worsened the dampness, as the stone walls now covered with cement mortar couldn't breathe anymore. They also tell me that the original owners were two siblings, Marcus and Maggie, who lived there on their own. They had no road access, so their only access was by boat from the sea. They said that they felt their presence and that it gave them comfort on this otherwise lonely place.

I suggest that I will communicate with the energy of the place to get a deeper understanding of the cause of the dampness.

I meet the spirit of the deceased Marcus and Maggie outside the house on the north side between the shed and a place where Marcus used to sit and look out to the sea. I introduce myself and tell them that the current owners are so glad to have them and that they see their gratitude as a token of honouring the past. I ask them how they are. They tell me that they are sad because they are stuck.

They continue to tell me that they have grievances towards their relatives. These were ashamed of both of them. Maggie never married even though she was rather pretty, while Marcus was small and crippled. So the relatives left them the house with the worst land and no access by land. They had a hard and poor life. But the worst was being shunned and excluded by both the family and the community.

I ask them what they want now. They want to move on but need help and are grateful that I have come. I say that I would send them on to the higher vibrations where they would be happier. But first I would need to ask my clients and present owners for permission as they find comfort in their presence.

I ask them if the house was damp at their time. 'Well, there was an open fire and always a draft... No, it was not rendered' (meaning the stone walls were bare).

I say goodbye to them and promise that I will come back once my clients have agreed.

On the same day in the evening back in my own home in County Mayo I go on an inner journey:

I feel the two of them clinging on to me. They don't want to go back even when I command them. I feel an inner conflict between needing to ask my clients for permission and their demand to be liberated. I talk with them and tell them that they can't stay here with me, which they don't want either. Next I try to send them off to the light but without avail.

As I am working outside of our house the following day, I feel their presence very intensely.

They are back at my side again, ranting and raving, jumping up and down mad with rage. I tell them that I understand their anger and empathise with them. They never dared to express their anger before. They appear again a few times during the day and I assure them that they are loved and understood. By evening they are tired of their anger and ask me to send them off to the light, which I subsequently do. They are glad, thank me and have been gone since that day.

I went on this inner journey at home, which proves that the dimension I communicated with is independent of time and space and that energy is always present everywhere. Why was I not able to send them off the first time even though they asked me to? They first needed to vent their anger; something they were never able to express. What do I mean by "sending them off to the light"? I mean to raise their vibrations, the frequency of their energy field. By expressing their anger they released energy which was blocked even during their (physical) life time and now it could flow again.

What were the practical implications of this communication? The information I received made me aware of the fact that stone cottages always had a draft and the constant open fire always kept the house dry. Current standards to have the house so well insulated that no heating is needed, created a big conflict for me architecturally. The idea to wrap the house on all sides except the east with extensions solved the problem of damp walls and ceilings. Repairing a leaky gutter and digging a deeper drain on the south side, where the internal floor was lower than the ground level outside, eliminated the rising dampness on one wall.

My professional expertise and experience enabled me transform the energetic release into practical solutions. You may argue that any professional expert with experience would come up with the same solutions. However by connecting with the energy of the place and bringing it back into flow, I am now working with the full support of the place. There is a living relationship with the place, which creates a joy and ease and a sense of mystery such as exists between two lovers. There is no separation between the place and me, between me as an architect and a human being. The more layers and dimensions of reality we are in contact with, the deeper and fuller our life becomes.

In the consequent process of designing an extension for the house, I got in contact with the personality of the place.

Captain of the ship
  On the edge between land and sea
    Transforming light into lower frequencies.

Before designing the extension of the house, I journeyed to ask the spirit of the place for advice and support. It reveals itself in the image of a water nymph, who likes to sit where the old inhabitants used to sit. She tells me that the owner of the house wants to be the captain and in charge of the planning and design process. She tells me to jump into the sea with her to become one with her. We swim in curves into darkness. She lives in a white light bubble under the sea. She catches the light and transforms it into another frequency. I now see more curves in the house design, a kind of cave behind the stairs and more details which will support my design. Her name is Melinda. I shall call her, when I design or work on the house.

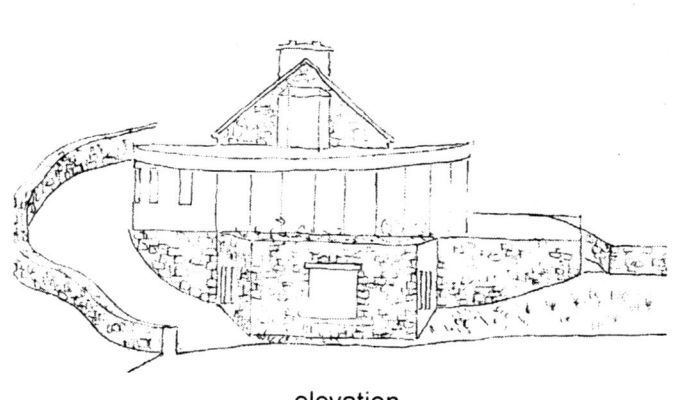

elevation

I consequently included the client even more in the design process. In this way we finally reached agreement on a design idea, which has expressed the presence of both the earth and the sea with a living room shaped like a ship and the rectangular bedrooms covered with a green roof. From a bay window from his study he can look out from the first floor as the captain of the ship.

However, by the time the design plans were finalised, the financial crisis and the consequent collapse of the building industry shocked the whole country. As a consequence my clients could not sell their house, whose sale would have funded the restoration and extension of this house.

Earth and sky,
  Land and sea,
    Creative tension
To reconcile opposing forces.

5 years later, while writing this book, I wondered about the essence of the place. The inner journey to answer this question revealed the following:

When I arrive at the place, the earth starts moving at one point and a snake moves outwards and upwards. She faces me calling for my attention. At first I am afraid of her venom, but she wraps herself around my body in a friendly embrace, unfurls again and stretches further upwards towards the sky. She tells me that the purpose of the place is to connect to the life energy within (in India called kundalini energy) by connecting to the earth and the sky in order to grow from the inside out. The place, located on the edge between the sea and land, brings forth creativity to reconcile opposite forces. The energy of the place can support the couple who live there to grow from within and use their opposite qualities to grow and unite. The isolation of the place, far removed from other people, fosters this inner work and growth.

site plan

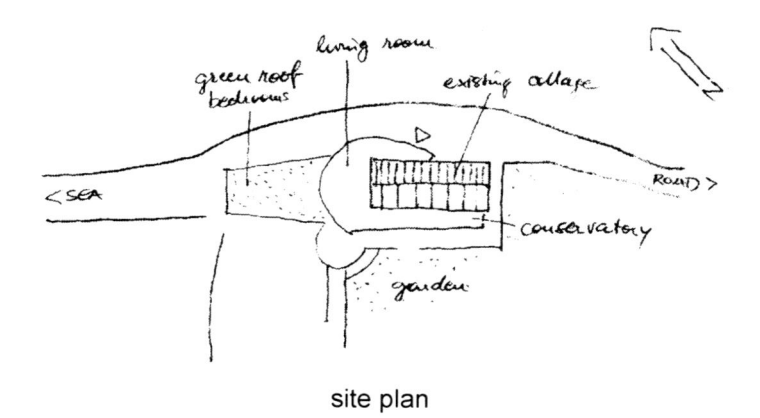

In hindsight it is interesting that I had already intuitively, after the first contact, picked up an aspect of the essential quality of the place by wrapping the extension like a snake around the existing cottage.

Castle in Dublin, Ireland

Bring the light of awareness into existing power structures.
  But are the owners and caretakers
    ready for a new outlook
      and willing to change?

The house was built at the end of the 18th century in Georgian style with the front extended in the 19th century. It was originally built by an Irish man who took part in the uprising against the English in 1798. In the middle of the 20th century it was divided up into apartments. The present owners use it as a family home after they have restored the original layout.

As the children had grown up and the house became too big and too expensive to run, I was approached with the question what to do with it.

My inner journey to find an answer to this question, provided the following answer:

I see within the space of the curved central hall and staircase a big vortex. The energy of the vortex originates from a lay line, which connects to a university and an important public building. The purpose of the building is to bring the light of awareness into power structures and their representatives, in order to remove barriers and divisions, which all have their source in our mind.

It needs new institutions, which prepare the way for the future. The owner is familiar with existing power structures and their short comings. His wife brings purity and innocence into the process. By working together the couple can offer and hold the space. Even though she is not involved at the moment, she brings an important aspect to the process.

The crisis in state and church demands new thinking, questioning of existing structures and power houses, that will encourage new pathways and a process of chaos, uncertainty and emptiness from which new and fresh ideas can emerge.

The owners are the keepers of this space, the gate keepers. They hold the vision.

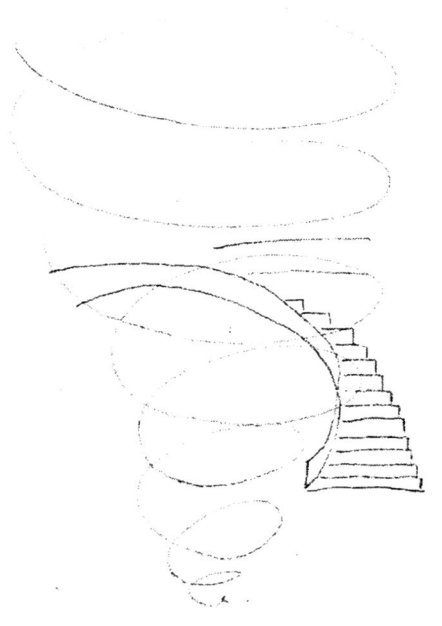

Vortex in vestibule

For the following two years we worked together. Renovations were started, the basement cleared. The big dining hall was transformed into a workshop space. Workshops from yoga to poetry and creative writing, parties with healthy food and mediation sessions were held. Two of the children moved back in. The old and the new are in conflict with each other, sometimes in a seemingly chaotic yet creative manner. Transformation is taking place.

ENERGIES OF HIGHER FREQUENCY

A house in County Mayo, Ireland, now called Essence of Mulranny

When mind and feelings are connected,
   Cheerful can belly dance
      and the road will stretch into the horizon and beyond.

Bettina wanted to bring an American poet to the West of Ireland. We had taken part in one of her workshops in the East of the country and were both fascinated by her teachings and approach to poetry. While we were looking for a place big enough for a group to gather, which could offer food and accommodation, we got in contact with the owner of this house in Mulranny. We visited her and were overwhelmed by the stunning view over Clew Bay to Croagh Patrick (in ancient times called Eagle Mountain) on the far side of the bay. I suggested going on an inner journey to get in contact with the spirit of the place.

The Spirit is full of life, very happy. I call her 'Cheerful'. The energy suggests building a fireplace next to her statue and performing ceremonies four times a year or even every month. She has called us together and while I am aware of her, she is now also connected to our home near Castlebar and to two other places I have connected with recently. She asks me to focus on the spot where the fireplace will be. I see the male owner of the house and hear the call to connect mind and feelings. I see a road stretching into the horizon and beyond as I fly along. I see cheerful dancing, like belly dancing. Or do I see Cheerful belly dancing? Most importantly I see the road as a path, a spiritual path. The woman who owns the house together with her husband is the cheerful spirit.

It is very interesting that the artist who built the statue outside the house was in contact with the spirit of the place and brought it into form. The road stretching into the horizon represents the teaching potential this place, not only for this couple who lives there, but also for groups of people who came and will come in the distant future (as the road stretches into the horizon and beyond). Croagh Patrick, when seen from Westport, has a masculine quality with its conical shape reaching into the sky. From this place I see a pregnant woman, the feminine receiving life-giving aspect of this holy mountain of Ireland.

Five years later this place has accommodated many workshops, including five weeklong poetry workshops. In the meantime another building has been added, which includes further accommodation and a workshop for bead-making and other crafts. The women of the community meet there to make cushions, rugs, gloves and pieces of art from sheep wool, which would otherwise be dumped by farmers as it is not profitable for them to sell the wool.

The village has recently won a "European Destinations of Excellence Award", the old railway line has been transformed into a cycle and walk way. The village is growing and thriving as the 'Essence of Mulranny' is radiating into the village and the wider community.

Shangri-La, Co. Mayo, Ireland

Be aware of our presence.
  Don't just step in.
    Heed the threshold!
      We are benign.

The same owner asked me a few years later to make a feasibility study on a land close to her house. The land in question has 3.5 acres and is divided into two sites with one cottage on each. The north facing site was called Shangri-La by the owners who built the house in the 1940s. There is a cottage with a hip roof and an extension to the rear on the south facing site. The owner's intention was to develop both sites for the purpose of supporting arts, science and nature, and that each of these areas learns to communicate and cooperate with each other.

While connecting with the spirit of the land, it turned out that three steps were required to connect to the place on an energetic level.

On my first visit I enter the land at the gate that leads through a tunnel of rhododendron bushes and hit my head against a cut off branch. I feel called to stop. The energy of the place says: "Be aware of our presence. Don't just step in! Heed the threshold! We are benign. We just ask for awareness and respect, which comes naturally once you are aware of our presence. We want to communicate with humans, but you need to calm down, align with your innermost centre and ask for contact... Now you are ready to continue walking the land. Let yourself be guided and know that you are now connected with us." I ask: "Who is us?". The answer is: "Wait. This is not about a name. Get to know us by feeling and sensing us and then you give us whatever name is most suited according to the information you receive".

After this communication I walked the land, took in all the information the owner gave me, without forming any conclusions or developing any ideas of what could be done with the land. This focused intention allowed me to keep my head empty and stop my mind interfering.

The following day I meditate in my office after asking the energy of the place for advice with regard to the development of the place. I consequently see myself on the place lying face down on the earth. I see myself getting up and feel an energetic entity standing in front of me, barring my way.

After the meditation I know that I first have to connect deeper with the energy. I am to go to the place and lie down as I have done in the meditation.

When I visit the land again, I lie down on the ground in the pathway/tunnel leading to the house. I go on an inner journey with the intention of connecting and communicating with the spirit of the place. I feel an energetic connection as being pulled right down into the earth without any verbal communication or any visual images informing me. When I get up I hear a lively buzzing sound all around me. I start walking the land again and this time a unified concept for the future development of the place unfolds as I proceed in my walk.

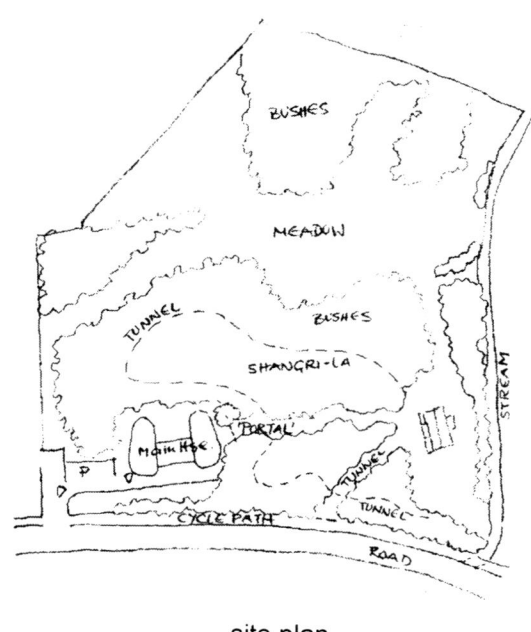

site plan

There are tall bushes along the road of Shangri-La (according to Wikipedia Shangri-La is a fictional place, a mystical harmonious valley described by James Hilton. It has become synonymous with an earthly paradise, a permanent 'happyland', isolated from the outside world). These tall bushes serve as a protective shield against the outside world. As experienced in other locations, place names are very often intuitively chosen to express the energy of a place.

The energy of the southern site is very different. Here are the views open to both the sea and the holy mountain on the other side of the bay. I envisage the entrance to the place on this site, both by car and on foot. The space around the house could be widened to allow for an extension to the existing house. This extension should be designed in such a way as to express both the mystery and the essence of nature, in contrast to the existing building with its straight lines and rectangular angles, which represents the rational, logical aspect of science. The existing entrance (through tunnel created by rhododendrons) should be closed.

The pathway from this building to the Shangri-La building should be winding and swinging to encourage a sense of awareness and wonder in those entering the site. I suggest narrow tunnels running through the dense Rhododendron area on both sides connecting to this winding pathway. These tunnels could widen in some parts, providing an area of rest and be so low in other parts that one has to crawl through. Art objects formed from pieces of the natural environment could be placed along the pathways.

This project could encourage a more balanced approach from everyone, not just scientists, to open their intuitive side. The workshop and meeting places would then encourage and facilitate a dialogue between scientists, artists and lay people with nature providing a bridge between two apparently opposing world views.

County Mayo, Ireland

An old ring fort,
  a light vortex,
    a home for nature spirits.

Yesterday I went to the lake in the nearby town. The holy mountain, Croagh Patrick, can be seen in the distance. The local authority has just built a new bridge between two lakes. At the same time a new footpath was built all around the lake. A boat brings us to the centre of the lake and I am surprised how light the energy feels as the energy around the lake always felt very dark and heavy. Patients from the nearby mental hospital used to go there and drown themselves in the lake.

Some years ago I was asked as an architect to make a suggestion for the best use of the land north of the lake. I discovered an old ring fort which turned out to be both a light vortex and a home for nature spirits. I consciously connected to this energy vortex for a period of time. The plots of land were subsequently sold to the town council and turned into a park as I had suggested. I followed an inner calling to pray that the bridge be built over the lake despite the economic downturn.

On a physical level there is just a new bridge, a park and new footpaths. When the bridge was opened this weekend by the arts council and the mayor of the town, no one was aware of the other realms/dimensions that had prepared this physical manifestation. Every physical manifestation first needs to be prepared on an invisible, astral level. I did this by connecting to the energy of the lake and the ring fort via thoughts, intentions, visualisations and visits on a regular basis for well over a year.

A year later a cafe has opened in the adjacent holiday village. A swimming pool with outdoor sport facilities is planned and a cycle and walking path between two towns is currently being built, starting at the lake.

Place on Achill Island, County Mayo, Ireland

Colours and shapes
                        constantly changing.
Deep silence
              in the everlasting now.

The roar of the sea,
continuous, never ending wind,
the spray of waves gushing in ecstasy
as they crash against the rocks.
Constantly forming and dissolving clouds.
And in all this movement-
stillness dropping deeper,
ever deeper into the earth.
Low tide – high tide.
Breathing out –
breathing in and out again.

These were the thoughts streaming through me as I sat behind a big glass window-pane looking out to the open Atlantic. Mothers used to give birth to their children in a house in this place. Why here, in this remote corner of Achill Island, the most western island of Ireland?

The clients and owners of the house made me aware of a fallen standing stone close to their house. These standing stones were used by the Celts to bring down and store universal energy. During one of my visits, when I stayed for a few days on my own in the house to look after their cat and plants, I connected with the energy of the site and got a deeper understanding of its energy and purpose.

I sense a circular energy field above the house, some 300 meter in diameter. It contains the blueprint for the whole island and is its gate keeper. Achill means eagle in Gaelic and is energetically connected to Croagh Patrick, which in pre-Christian times was called Eagle Mountain. The intelligence/energy of this place tells me to walk the land in order to connect to the place more deeply. When I walk the land afterwards, I become aware of a huge rock overhang facing the sea, which receives and stores the information from the energy field above. Later, as I sit in the house, I am pulled down into the earth and into deep silence. The essence of the place is the paradox between the ever changing sea, wind, colours, light and shadows; and the ever present silence of eternity. And isn't that the essence of life? We are in this world, to remember the timeless, spaceless and formless reality among the turmoil of our ever changing world.

And doesn't that give the answer to the question, why babies were born and blessed in this remote spot of a remote island? What better form of baptism could there be?

9. HOME

We are now coming to an end of our inner journey into hidden, invisible layers of a vast and boundless reality. At the same time this is also the beginning of a never-ending journey, about our connection with the earth and the universe. Once we have opened the door into the invisible reality of energy, we have set out on an adventure into our own inner universe.

I remember building our own house here in Ireland during our second year living here. We had moved the caravan out of the timber structure we had built the previous year and started to build the shell of our living room. All my efforts were directed at moving into the house by the end of the year. I did not want to live another winter in the caravan. I longed for a house which would give me shelter and protection from the rain and storms. As we built it in timber, I loved the play of light and shadows as the sun streamed into the inner space through the beams and posts of future walls and ceilings.

When we were ready to cover both walls and ceiling with timber boards and felt, I still remember the deep disappointment I experienced as the space got darker with every board we added. I was completely confused. Had I not achieved what I was striving for during the last few months? It was only years later that I understood the cause of my disappointment. This house was not the home I was looking for. The part in me striving for survival was now satisfied, but my soul was not. My soul was asking me to look for this home deep inside myself. And what an adventure into unknown, into forgotten worlds it became and continues to be.

When I was a student I loved to travel the world, see other cultures, buildings, cities and landscapes. And it was an adventure for me back then. But I did not realize that I was only scratching the surface. I was only exploring tiny parts of a small percentage of reality. And back then it was a huge step into unknown worlds to travel as a couple with a rucksack to the USA, South America and North Africa.

Exploring our inner universe, i.e. the interplay between the material and the spiritual, the visible and the invisible, becomes a symphony of different layers of reality adding their flavour and colour and their own unique sound. It is best to meet life in this multidimensional world with a sense of wonder, because we only understand it in hind side. We can only marvel with a sense of gratitude at what seems chaotic. Were it not for our ideas of how reality should be, we would see perfect order and harmony instead of chaos.

So when the home we are longing for can only be found within us, why all the fuss and explanations about energies of places? As we need both a body and a soul in order to live, laugh and love, we also need the connection to both the earth and the sky. We only exist in relationship to the energies all around us, both visible and invisible. To enter into an intimate relationship with the place and space we inhabit is only one way of connecting with all these multidimensional energies. The more we enter deep intimate relationships with our partner, children, friends, animals, plants, the earth or with our car, a canvas, an instrument (the list is endless), the deeper we can relate to ourselves, the more we will feel alive, fulfilled, happy and at peace. We are truly at home at last!

I thank you for journeying with me for a while. I thoroughly enjoyed your company and I wish you well on your own journey into your vast, inner universe.

For a personal consultation or workshops please contact me by email: gpeterseil@hotmail.com

ENDNOTES

[1] "Feng Shui is a Chinese geomantic practice in which a structure or site is chosen or configured so as to harmonize with the spiritual forces that inhabit it." www.merriam-webster.com "Feng Shui is based on the Taoist vision and understanding of nature, particularly on the idea that the land is alive and filled with Chi, or energy." www.fengshui.about.com, also Karen Kingston, Creating Sacred Space with Feng Shui, Broadway Books, 1997

[2] Handbook of Vastu Shastra, B. Niranjan Babu, 1997, UBS Publishers Distributors, India, www.ubspd.com

[3] "Shamanism is an ancient spiritual tradition...used...for healing, problem solving and for maintaining balance between humans and nature". "Scandinavian Center for Shamanic Studies". www.shamanism.dk

[4] "Geomancy means divination by means of figures or lines or geographic features, Merriam Webster Dictionary, www.merriam-webster.com "Geomancy explores the realm where human consciousness meets and dialogues with the Spirit of the Earth. It empowers the harmonious interaction between person and place..." Mid-Atlantic Geomancy, www.geomancy.org

[5] "Quantum Physics is a branch of science that deals with discrete indivisible unites of energy called quanta as described by the Quantum Theory." www.library.thinkquest.org

[6] Fallingwater, 2012 calender, www.fallingwater.org

[7] Ratu Bagus, www.ratubagus.com

[8] Option Dialogue Process, www.option.org

[9] Jill Bolte Taylor's stroke of insight/Video on TED.com, www.ted.com/talks

[10] Marko Pogacnik, www.markopogacnik.com

ENDNOTES

[11] John G. Bennett, Energies, Material, Vital, Cosmic, Claymont Communications, 1989, www.jgbennett.net
[12] Google: Earth chakras, or go to: www.earthchakras.org/locations
[13] Dr. Raymond Moody, Life after Life, 1975, Mockingbird Books, also www.ThinkingAllowed.com Life after Life,
[14] "Ley lines are alleged alignments of a number of places of geographical and historical interest... The phrase was coined in 1921 by the amateur archaeologist Alfred Watkins...in his books "Early British Trackways" and "The Old Straight Track". www.wikipedia.org
[15] Scandinavian Center for Shamanic Studies, www.shaman-center.dk
[16] Vortex, Merriam-Webster Dictionary defines it as "a mass of spinning air, liquid, etc., that pulls things into its center. The Free Online Dictionary:...2. any activity, situation, or way of life regarded as irresistibly engulfing.